# Hansi

# Hansi

## captive of the swastika

by

Maria Anne Hirschmann

KINGSWAY PUBLICATIONS
EASTBOURNE

Copyright © 1973 by Tyndale House
Publishers, Wheaton, Illinois, U.S.A.

First printing June 1973

First British paperback edition 1974
Reprinted 1977
Reprinted 1979

ISBN 0 902088 60 2

Printed in Great Britain for
KINGSWAY PUBLICATIONS LTD.,
Lottbridge Drove, Eastbourne,
East Sussex BN23 6NT by
Hunt Barnard Printing Ltd,
Aylesbury, Bucks.
Composition by Hazell Watson & Viney Ltd,
Aylesbury, Bucks.

# Contents

# I

# An Orphan for Hitler

Mother bent over my straw bed. I looked up at the questioning, grey-blue eyes in her kind, wrinkled face.

"Mother, I whispered, "can I have a bowl of sauerkraut, please?"

Mother nodded and turned away. She ducked her grey head to avoid the low doorframe of the cottage's only bedroom. Because I was sick with an upset stomach, Mother had bedded me there on the wooden floor beside her own bed.

I listened to her quick steps moving away and followed her in my mind through the kitchen out to the stone-built storeroom by the goat stable. I could picture her every movement, for I had followed her there many times. She would enter the windowless room, light a candle, and set the burning light carefully on a rock. She always feared that our straw-thatched cottage might burn some day. She would lift out the big sandstone from the top of the barrel, remove a piece of board, and move the mouldy top layer of the sauerkraut aside. Then she would fill a bowl full of the crisp, cool sauerkraut which I had helped to prepare in the autumn.

The kitchen door banged again, and I heard her open a drawer for a fork. My mouth began to water. I had not eaten for two days, and all at once I felt hungry. Then I heard Father's voice.

"Don't spoil her so much, Anna; she mustn't have every whim fulfilled. She is trouble enough as it is."

"She is only a little child yet, Father." Mother's voice was quiet. "She only began school last year. She has been very patient through the whole day while I was busy working. She needs something to settle her stomach. God knows there isn't much fancy food in this house to spoil her, even when she is sick."

She pushed the bedroom door open and put the bowl and fork beside my makeshift bed on the floor.

"Mother," I asked, "can I go back to the hayloft tonight, please?"

She pondered for a moment. "But what if you need me? Do you feel well enough to be alone above? What if I don't hear you when you call?"

"I am fine, Mother." I lowered my voice to a scared whisper. "You know Father doesn't like it when I am around him. And I'd rather sleep in my own bed in the hay, really, Mother."

I tried to eat the sauerkraut, one of my favourite foods in healthy days, but Father's remark had spoiled the taste. I gave it back to Mother. Without another word she moved me up to my usual sleeping quarters. She tucked another blanket over my featherbed to keep out the winter's chill. The roof was brittle and draughty.

"Mother," I asked her as I often had before, "why doesn't Father like me? He doesn't scold when Sepp asks for hot chocolate sometimes, and there is always just enough for him and I can't have any."

Mother sat down beside me for a moment. This was a rare thing for one who always seemed to fly everywhere because there was so much to do in the fields or the stable. If not that, then she had to cook another meal at the big stone hearth heated by wood she gathered herself. But here she sat and seemed in no hurry.

"*Marichen* (little Mary), I have explained it before, but I will tell you again. When you were a little baby your mama brought you to us because she was very sick. She asked me if I would keep you until she was well again. Your mama and I were good friends, so I agreed to keep you for a while though it wasn't easy for us to do so. You know how scarce food and clothing are. Father had his hands full as a bricklayer to feed our own four children."

I nodded and watched the lantern draw ghostly shadows on the dark hay bales. I knew already what she would say next.

"When your mama died I decided to keep you, and Father wanted to adopt you, but your own papa would not give his permission. That made Father bitter. Now he thinks you don't belong here because Herr Appelt, your papa, could take you away from us anytime he wishes to do so."

Fear gripped my stomach. As I had so often before, I begged again, "Mother, don't let him take me away from here, please! I will hide in the woods if he comes! Please, Mother!"

"Don't worry, child, he will never come for you. He has forgotten you. He has never visited you even once since your mama laid you down on the wooden bench beside the stove and left you here. He is a proud man who gives himself fancy airs though he is poorer than a church mouse. Your dear mama died so young because she wouldn't listen, but married that mean fellow anyway. He put her into that early grave!"

She rose abruptly and picked up the flickering lantern. "Do not kneel beside your bed tonight, girl. It is too cold and you are well tucked in. Fold your hands and pray."

I closed my hands and drawled, "*Müde bin ich, geh zur Ruh* (tired I am and go to rest)." This was a common German prayer and I used it whenever I didn't want to pray in my own words as I knew Mother preferred me to do.

Saying a simple "Good night," Mother climbed down the steep ladder to the ground and left me alone, staring into the darkness.

I loved the loft, though I was always a little scared at being there alone in the dark. I breathed deeply to inhale the sweet fragrance of our mountain hay which I had missed for a night. I looked out of the small gable window waiting for the moon.

The moon was my friend. He chased away my fear and the murky gloom of night. Then I didn't feel alone. Besides, since the beginning of my second school year, the moon had become my ally against my foster father.

Father had forbidden me to read for more than one hour any evening. He took the oil lamp away, often in the middle of an interesting sentence, and sent me off to bed. There was no way of protesting. We children were brought up to be seen, not heard.

My rebellious spirit had found a way to defy him. I always hid a school book under my pillow and I knew exactly when the moon turned into a round face every month. But tonight I didn't feel like reading, though the full moon reflected the white shimmer of the snow with an unearthly brightness. I felt too upset. My stomach might have been full of butterflies. Tears washed across my cheeks, getting my ears wet and cold. I had touched the sorest spot of my young life—one that Mother avoided unless I asked.

I would never forget the moment when I heard her explain it to me for the first time. Still very young then, I had been quarrelling with Sepp, the youngest son of the house, three years older than I. He had been teasing me as he so often did, till I lost my temper and began to hammer his back with my small fists, yelling and screaming at him.

Suddenly he had turned around and said, "Look, sis! Save your breath and get lost! Don't you know that you aren't even my sister? I'm the real son here and you are just a nobody, an orphan. My mother is not your mother, either!"

I stared into his grinning face and shouted, "I am going right now and tell Mother what you said. And you are going to get in trouble!"

"Go and tell! She is *my* mother, not yours, you *Dummkopf*. Go ahead, tell her!" Sepp triumphed.

Storming into the kitchen I threw my arms around Mother's waist and wailed, "Sepp is lying, isn't he, Mother? He said you aren't my mother!"

That's when she had to tell me for the first time that I didn't belong to that family. But as she finished she said, "Now you are my girl, *Marichen*, and I will keep you as long as they let me."

Since that day the shadow of a great worry had hung in my heart. Would they ever take me away from Mother?

I folded my hands and closed my eyes.

"Dear Jesus, don't let papa come and take me away, please! Bless Mother and Sepp and the others and—" I hesitated for a long moment, "—bless Father, too. Help me to be good so he will like me. Send my guardian angel by my bed. Amen."

When I opened my eyes I tried again my favourite but always unsuccessful trick. Mother, who had taught me how to pray, had also told me that God and the angels could not be seen. But I was certain they must become visible whenever I closed my eyes. So I always tried to open my eyes very slowly or so fast after prayer that I might catch a glimpse of the heavenly visitors before they disappeared again. I was never fast enough to catch even the last shimmer of an angel wing. Now even the moon had passed the little window and my loft was scary and dark.

Papa never came, but spring did. Then summer and autumn and winter again in quiet steadiness from year to year. As time passed my love for Mother grew deeper, but my resentment grew stronger towards my foster father and my papa whom I had never seen. I had learned to blame him for all my troubles, which were plenty.

Father, a short, thin-faced man with a black moustache, had strict ideas about his household. He, the patriarch, reigned with an iron hand. His wife and children submitted silently— except for me. My proud, unbroken stubbornness clashed countless times with his hard demands. He tried various ways to subdue me—by leather belt, by locking me for a whole day in the dark storeroom with scurrying mice, by making me go hungry.

I never dared to answer back when he scolded. I knew better than that. But my set jaw, clenched fists, and blazing eyes signalled temper and rebellion clearly enough. Often I provoked him into fits of rage, and the whole family suffered because of it.

Poor little Mother! She was the go-between from year to year and the tongue-lashings she endured so often for my stubborn sake were my greatest and most painful punishments. Only her pleading, tearful eyes had been able to melt my uncompromising rebellion—but less so as I approached my early teen years.

Only for Mother I would sometimes apologize; I could do anything for her—but only for her. I knew my presence was like acid to my Father's ulcered stomach. But he was poison for my stomach also, and together we were a taxing drain on Mother's tired heart.

One reason I loved spring and summer so much was that it was then possible to stay out of Father's way more often. The hard, long winters in the Sudeten mountains of Czechoslovakia forced people close to the little pipe stove and elbows rubbed easily. But when the little brook began to murmur under the melting snow and the brave, fragile snowdrops pierced the

night-crusted wet snow with their little pointed stems, herald-
ing the rebirth of another spring, my joy grew boundless.

Nobody could find snowbells—as Mother called her favourite flowers—earlier than I, and Mother's eyes misted happily
when I brought her the first flowers of the year. As soon as she
let us go out without shoes, my easy time began.

I spent countless happy hours gathering wild berries and
mushrooms in the shady coolness of the dark green forest that
came up to our back windows. I romped with the little spring-
born goats and picked dandelions for their gentle mothers. I
feared the bees, but loved their hum in the blossoming fruit
trees. I whistled with the starlings and picked forget-me-nots
for Mother. And I avoided the house when Father was home.

Harvest time brought hard work for all of us. I was so thin
and small; Mother's eye would sometimes be on me when I
tried to straighten my tired back, and ever so often she found an
excuse to send me in to easier work. But she toiled on and on,
weeding, cultivating, digging winter potatoes, baling hay, pulling cabbage, and all the while silently accepting Father's
criticism for over-protecting me.

Autumn brought brown, ploughed empty spots around the
house. I hated the colour brown, which became to me a symbol
of new confinement to the house with Father around. My two
favourite colours, blue and green, vanished. The blue sky
turned grey with clouds, and the green pastures were bare and
ready for deep blankets of snow. As nature went to sleep, I
often longed to be one of Father's bees that wintered in.

But one autumn, September 1938, brought new colours,
symbols, and changes of pace into my life. On a sunny autumn
day when the leaves burned red splashes into the deep blue
skies, strange soldiers marched down the country road bearing
a flag redder than the most flaming leaf. In the middle of the
flag was a white circle with a black cross. But what a cross! It

had hooks on all four ends. The soldiers sang as they waved that flag. Horses and riders, tanks and cannons poured over the mountain ridge, and our little German village held its breath and skipped a heartbeat while the inhabitants watched from behind the windows and waited.

They didn't have to wait long. Almost at once the army loudspeakers announced the peaceful intentions of Hitler who had sent the army to "free" the German brothers "oppressed" by the Czech government since the disgraceful Verdict of Versailles of 1918. The army train was bringing not only a *Gulasch-kanone* (field kitchen), but a whole new future for everybody. So people dared to step outdoors and the children were first to make friends with the smiling soldiers.

Mother watched for a long time and listened carefully to all the announcements and messages over the loudspeaker. Soon we all knew the whole story. Adolf Hitler, Germany's Fuhrer, had sent his troops to make Sudetenland part of the Third Reich. Hitler pledged his word that hunger, unemployment, and hardship were over for everybody.

Mother nodded thoughtfully, then murmured softly, "Maybe Jesus sent that man Hitler into our land to bring an end to the depression. Things couldn't get any worse than they are now!"

And things did not get any worse; there was much improvement right from the start.

Father had longer hours of work at better pay. He seemed more pleasant—at least for a while. School got more exciting, too. The Nazi party brought many gifts from Germany into our poor community, and the gift I enjoyed most was several boxes of new school library books for the unlimited use of anybody in our tiny country school. I read and read and read— and Father raged again!

My teacher, a secret follower of Hitler for years, became

overnight the acknowledged hero of the village, and everybody sought his friendship and advice.

It didn't take Hitler's troops marching into Czechoslovakia to make my teacher an object of hero-worship in my eyes. He and I had been on best of terms for a long time. I was his right-hand helper in the one-room school, tutoring primary students while he taught the upper grades. After school I baby-sat for his children without pay. He encouraged my passion for reading just as Mother did.

Mother had nothing new for me to read any more. I had already read every printed page in the cottage several times, even Mother's Bible and the hymnbook.

Teacher gave much of his own time to advance me scholastically, and one day it became clear to me why he pushed me so hard. Not too long after Czechoslovakia became a protectorate of the Third Reich, Nazi educators began testing every student. Along with thousands of other teenagers, I accepted the challenge. Yes, I would pass those tests. I would show everybody that students of simple country schools were as smart as city kids. *Herr Lehrer* (Mister Teacher) laid his hands on my shoulders and said, "I know you can do it, Maria! You can make it to the top!'

What top? I soon found out. Hitler was picking young people all over the country for special training in Nazi schools. They were selected by special qualifications, not by force. It was a privilege and an honour to qualify. After the first two tests it stopped being a game for me. It became hard work and stiffest competition. By the time I had been selected to represent my county in the next testing-round for the entire Sudetenland, I felt scared. The county supervisor tried to prepare me gently.

"Maria, your teacher is very proud of you and so are we. But now you are matching yourself against the top students of many counties. I hope you will not be too disappointed if you are not selected. From this testing camp only a very few will be sent to Prague to be specially trained for Nazi youth leadership. It is next to impossible for an untrained mountain girl like you to make the top."

That did it! Yes, I knew I was only a skinny peasant girl who looked like a boy except for the long blonde pigtails. I knew how clumsy I was, too, and that I had never been in a county office before. But to call me "untrained"—well, that was a polite way of calling me dumb. That was a challenge! I *would* make the top! And so I did.

When I returned to my own school after ten days in testing camp, my classmates stood up and cheered. So did *Herr Lehrer*, and I thought I saw his eyes become moist. Even Father smiled, and my head whirled!

To think that a poor orphan girl such as I would have such luck! I had been chosen from among many thousands of students to be further educated in one of Hitler's special schools. It was a great honour. On top of that, I would go to Prague, the capital of my homeland—a place I had longed to see ever since I had been able to read. I had never dared to dream that big, and had never seen anything beyond our small county town. I bubbled over with joy, and the envy of the village people made me lift my head high.

The only one who did not rejoice with me was Mother. She packed my meagre belongings, and during my remaining days at home her tired shoulders hung lower than usual as in her quiet, quick way she tended to the many tasks of a hardworking, frugal cottage woman.

She looked burdened and helpless in an unspoken grief. It puzzled me, but it was not my place to ask questions.

The struggle for survival has furrowed deep wrinkles into the faces and hearts of the people of the Sudeten Mountains. They are sparing of words and diffident in display of affection. For me to ask the cause of Mother's sorrow would be unthinkable.

She called me before sunrise on the day of my departure. She had the customary bread, soup, and potatoes ready before I had my long hair brushed and braided. Then we loaded my large, rope-tied, wooden box on the small rack wagon, and knelt down for prayer before we left the house. Then Mother kissed me. Kisses were shy, awkward, and only for those who left home for good. She had so kissed each of the four older children when they left. Now I too was leaving, the last fledgling to fly from the nest.

Without speaking, we pulled the wagon up the little hill past our brown, ploughed-under rye field, past the partially harvested potatoes. Then Mother stopped.

"Turn around, child," she said. "Look once more before you leave home. Childhood is waving farewell and you are stepping out today into a big, wide world. But there will never be anything more precious than this spot, be it ever so simple, for it was your home."

Tears filled my eyes. Mother could sound so poetic and wise on special occasions. I stopped to turn and look. How I loved the little white cottage beneath the big cherry trees! Would I ever see it again? Would I ever hear the tall fir trees sing again in the morning wind? Would I ever lie among the wildflowers in the soft grass, watching the summer clouds sail past, and dreaming young dreams?

"Mother," I asked softly, "will Father ever permit me to come back to visit? He didn't even shake my hand to bid me farewell this morning. I know he is glad I am leaving. He doesn't think this is my home. You are the only one who made it home for me. Now that I'm leaving, Father is closing the door on me, isn't he?"

Mother didn't answer, and her short, laboured breathing told me that her heart was giving her trouble again. She didn't need upsetting thoughts. We both reached for the rope and moved on. I did not let myself look back even one last time after that.

2

The only way to live with this most sensitive spot in my soul was to ignore it. And after all, did I not walk toward a great new future?

I was the only passenger who climbed onto the old cannon-ball, and as the conductor helped me with my box the train whistle shrilled impatiently while the sooty locomotive started to hiss and smoke. I stood at the open train window, smiling down into Mother's sad eyes.

Sparks and cinders flew around her small figure. The morning wind loosened stray wisps of her thin white hair which was combed straight back into a tightly-braided bun. Her expression puzzled me. Her eyes held the kind of agony I had seen only twice as long as I lived with her. Into my excitement and anticipation crept a strange, foreboding fear as I wondered why she looked so troubled.

The first time I had seen that helpless look was when she had told me I had been born of another mother—that bitter moment when my world had broken apart and we suffered together.

The second time I had seen the same agony in her eyes was only a few months before I left home. Just a year after Hitler's troops occupied Czechoslovakia, war began. All the young men were called to bear arms. Sepp, Mother's youngest son, was drafted. It was not the parting that concerned Mother the most. She knew that men must go to war. Every generation in Europe followed this pattern. Grandfather had fought in the Franco-Prussian War—Father served several years during World War I, just after he and Mother had married—now Sepp's turn had come. But after the first World War Mother had become convinced that her sons should not carry rifles and kill human beings. This was her great burden. She knew Hitler would make no exceptions for Sepp, for Nazi rules were iron rules. She was aware, too, that the village party leader considered her thinking dangerous and cowardly. "Heil Hitler" for everybody—that was it!

Sepp himself had not been disturbed about the matter as he made ready to leave. There were the daily radio announcements of victory from every fighting front, and he was young and strong and eager to win the war. He looked sharp in his new German uniform; and before he left, a girl in the village had whispered a sweet promise into his ear. The future belonged to him. After all, war would soon be over. But Mother seemed to know different as in choked grief she bade her boy good-bye.

Now why should Mother look at me in my hour of parting with the same heartrending anguish? I did not leave to go to war. Didn't she realize how lucky I was, how happy and eager I felt? This should not be a time for sorrow, but for rejoicing because I had been chosen! They had selected me, a nobody, an ugly duckling, to go to the new Nazi school in Prague after all those grinding tests. Someday I would be a youth leader for the Fuhrer. My honour in being selected would bring honour to her; I would make her proud of me. Why couldn't she rejoice with me?

The train jerked hard and began to move. Mother lifted her drawn face, stretched out her worn hands toward me and over the clatter called in a heart-strangled voice, "*Marichen, Marichen,* don't ever forget Jesus!"

I smiled and shouted back, "Don't worry, *Muetterlein* (Mother dear)! How could I ever forget you and God?"

I felt so relieved! Was *that* why she looked so perturbed? Why should Mother worry about such a simple matter? Hadn't she taught me to love God? Had I not prayed beside her from babyhood? Didn't I know my Bible. And what about the many hymns I knew by heart? We had sung them together in our garden veranda some evenings. Could I ever forget those precious moments of worship when the whole family would sit in the glow of sunset, and after Father had read from the Bible Mother's soft voice would start all of us singing, singing—until the neighbours would open their windows to catch a few strains of our little family choir. I tried to harmonize with Mother's melody, lower or higher, never taking my eyes from her face and kind eyes. I would never forget God, and to me God was like Mother and Mother like God. Whenever I prayed to my Friend, Jesus, I could picture him only with kind, blue-grey eyes like Mother's.

The train gathered speed and noise. In the receding distance stood a lonely, black-clad figure waving a white handkerchief. I waved and called, *Auf Wiedersehen!*" until the train rounded a curve and I saw her no more. The bright morning sun mounted a spruce-wooded hill hiding the view of the village and our cottage. A last time I strained out of the window to see the hills, the village, and the white cottage, but it was all gone, and at that moment it struck me that I would never see the place again. I swallowed the lump in my throat and fought tears just for a moment; then my eager anticipation took over and my heart began to sing again. I listened to the train wheels and they sang with me; "Let's go to Prague; let's go to Prague; let's go; let's go!"

## 2

# "Sieg Heil! Sieg Heil!"

Surely I was dreaming! I would wake up and find myself in my warm hayloft, rubbing my sleepy eyes and feeling disappointed that it was only a dream! How could it be true that I, a fourteen-year-old peasant girl, was permitted to be in Prague?

I stumbled from the train and dragged my box out, holding tightly to it and my coat. I felt dazed, helpless, scared, elated, and unbelievably fortunate. No, I did *not* dream. I had arrived in Prague!

*"Die Goldene Stadt"* (The Golden City), we German young people called Prague admiringly after a Nazi-produced movie featuring beautiful pictures of the city. But oh! She was so much fairer than her pictures. I fell in love with her that very first moment.

I stood for a while watching thousands of strangers surge to and fro in the busy, crowded depot. I had never seen so many people in a crowd before—how many people were there in the world? The masses moved me towards the gate and I wondered in which language I should ask for the way to the streetcar. I spoke German, my mother's tongue, and Czech also. Knowing how deeply the freedom-loving Czech people hated the German regime and the German language, I felt uncertain what to do.

Timidly I approached a uniformed official and began to inquire of him in German. I switched quickly to Czech as I noticed resentment in his polite face. He gave directions and soon I sat on a streetcar bench with my eyes searching out of the window. That was an unforgettable ride through a golden autumn afternoon.

I knew at once that afternoon which parts of Prague would be my favourites: The "Old Town," an idyllic part of the original settlement dating back to the ninth century; Charles Bridge, over 1600 feet long, dating from 1357, guarded by two massive towers adorned with statuary; the majestic Moldau River, the largest river of my country, spanned by twelve famous bridges.

"Mother Moldau," they call her because her waters mean fruitfulness and transportation for Bohemia. Unhurried, deep, and queenly she flows, carrying ships and boats under the old bridges, past flowery gardens and lovely parks.

I also saw sights of a different kind. As the antique streetcar rattled its long way through the streets and across brides, Hitler's bright red flags with the white circle and the black swastika waved in the autumn breeze from every great building and market place. Czech inscriptions had been painted over with German words. German soldiers, officers, and SS men thronged the sidewalks, for the pride of the Czech nation, called "Praha," had become the German city "Prag," and century-long traditions had been changed to please the German conquerors.

When at last I arrived at my school I wondered if I had lost my way and come to the wrong place. It didn't look like a a school. The gate opened into a small park, beautifully landscaped with fountains and statuary. Large trees bordered the walks and the entrance to the main building. The school itself was a white stone mansion. Wide, hand-carved wooden doors and slender, high windows gave it the appearance of a fairy-tale castle and I wondered if I would be allowed to enter. I waited for a few scary moments before I pulled the chimes and the friendly door opened wide.

After I had been registered and welcomed, I found my bed and *Spind*, as we called our wardrobes. Then I met some of my classmates. In the evening, feeling subdued and bashful, I sat busy with my own thoughts in the luxurious dining room where we would receive three simple meals a day. I learned that the mansion was the confiscated estate of an immensely wealthy Jew. The idea disturbed me. It still bothered me when I slipped quickly under the blankets of my bunk bed. The mattress felt strange—I was used to a strawbed. I also had the habit of saying my prayers beside my bed, but it would embarrass me to do that here! I wondered what Mother would think about all of it. The thought of the little Bible which I had found tucked among my stuff as I unpacked made me feel uneasy and confused. Weariness enveloped me and I wanted to dismiss all bothersome thoughts. Well, someday I hoped to understand it all.

Before long I found myself well adjusted to my new way of life and with youthful enthusiasm I faced my new opportunities. My shyness left me, and I bounced around as my usual confident self, ready to lead and to compete with the best of my class. I studied hard, learned to obey and salute in wordless summission, and soon received special recognition from the student body and faculty. I could forget that I had been an orphan girl dependent upon the mercy of a poor foster home; I felt accepted and needed.

Someone began to call me "Hansi"—I'll never know who started it. In just a matter of weeks even the teachers picked up my new nickname. It fitted so well! I was slim and bony, built like a boy. I acted like one, too, but everybody seemed to like me as I was, so I stopped worrying about my missing feminine curves and enjoyed life and my new name.

Each day the memories of my childhood faded a little more. It seemed as if I had never lived any other life than my new Nazi school life. Mother seemed very far away and almost unreal.

How I loved school! My teachers could bring everything to life. History fascinated me. People long dead stepped out of the pages of my Nazi history book and lived again for me. They became my friends, or enemies. They acted proud, heroic, or cowardly; they loved, fought, suffered, died. My vivid imagination lived and acted with them as my heart learned a new theme—"Adolf Hitler and the Third Reich."

Hitler was with us every hour, though he lived in Berlin and we in his school in Prague. His sayings were quoted in every class. His doctrines were our most important study. His book, *Mein Kampf,* lay under the nightlamp on every bedside table. Our teachers practically worshipped him. They would undoubtedly lay down their lives for him and the nation. All our instructors were young, picked for their enthusiasm, ability, and devotion to the party. Though they demanded obedience and strict self-discipline, they were kind, warm, understanding and fair.

One teacher I loved above all others—our music teacher. Slim, petite, always smiling, tastefully dressed, she wore her hair in blonde waves framing a pleasant oval face. Her main attraction was her eyes—big blue ones, true, firm, but understanding and kind.

Late one afternoon, several weeks after I had arrived at that school, I first decided Miss Walde was someone special. It had been an especially hard day, with many examinations. Our endurance had been tested, as it was so often, to our limit. Our last test had been scheduled in the music room, and we marched into that place feeling played out and nervous. The girls urged me to be first to try the oral test. I complied, grinning as I stepped up to the grand piano. The late afternoon sun streamed through the high windows and threw golden ornaments over my teacher, the instrument, and the soft oriental rug beneath it. The dark-panelled room seemed dusty and hot. My teacher asked me to sing a German folk song for her, one we had studied a few days before. I had been braced for some difficult requirement, and her gentle request threw me completely off. I threw my hands before my face and burst into tears. Before I could compose myself, the whole group of girl students sobbed with me, not knowing what to expect next.

The teacher turned on her piano stool in surprise. She waited, smiling, while I searched for my forgotten handkerchief, then she pulled a snow-white handkerchief out of her dress pocket and handed it to me. Deeply embarrassed over my emotional conduct, I dried my tears.

When each girl had found her composure again, Miss Walde stood up and laughed sweetly. Then she said, "You are dismissed! Go for a walk in the sunshine, do anything you please, and report on time for supper."

"But—what about our music test?" I stammered. "Did we all fail?"

"Oh, no," she said reassuringly, "you all passed. Go out now and relax. We will have some more tests on another day."

Shouting our *"Dankeschön,"* we hurried out of the music hall and stepped into the afternoon sun. Separating myself from the group, I went to my favourite spot of the estate, a white bench nestled among large lilac bushes. Even though the lilac was not in bloom, I loved that place because it was a hidden cosy nook. Whenever I needed solitude for my dreams or problems I would go to "my" bench. Trying to bring order to my stormy, puzzled thoughts, I stared at the dainty white handkerchief still in my tense hand, and relived the last hour in the music hall. What a teacher! How good and noble she had been! How understanding and generous! What could I do for her to show my gratitude? I knew what she would say.

"Little Hansi," she would say, "grow up pure and clean and give your life for the service of others, for our glorious Reich, and for our Fuhrer, and it will be enough reward for me as your teacher."

Yes, I would do what she expected. I would grow up to be like her, firm and dedicated. Her blue eyes puzzled me. I could not escape the feeling that I had seen those eyes before I came to Prague. But where? They were eyes I loved and respected. Where had I seen them before?

As time passed, Miss Walde and I developed a silent friendship. She could not show any preference to any student—that would have been unfair. But we both sensed that we were made to be friends. I studied hard for every subject, but music with her was a privilege, not work. She opened a new world to me. She slipped free tickets into my hand for concerts and opera. She lent me her books. She helped me over my stage fright when singing solos. She taught me the first steps in choir directing. Her blue eyes approved, disagreed, encouraged, and pushed. Only one doubt clouded my mind, perplexing me more and more urgently.

Among other subjects, we had one period daily of "Study of Semitism," taught by a young SS officer who had been disabled in battle. Every day he hammered into our minds the story of the Jews as the Nazi party saw it. Using *Der Stürmer,* an anti-Semitic newspaper, Hitler's *Mein Kampf,* even the Bible, he built a damning case against the Jews, maintaining that it was their destiny to become extinct.

I listened attentively, and in my heart a battle raged. I had been brought up with the Bible and prayer and faith in Jesus Christ. Nobody had challenged them. Now, listening to this teacher's convincing arguments, I felt puzzled. Something was wrong either with him or with me. I grew restless and uncomfortable as I tried to think the matter through. Miss Walde noticed that I seemed perplexed, and raised her eyebrows in silent question. I uncertainly shook my head; I could not talk about it. It pained so much that I would not open my heart to show the storm inside.

I still prayed once in a while as Mother had taught me. Of course, not on my knees as Mother's custom had been, but lying in my bed I would give God some of my sleepy thoughts. According to Mother's religion, prayer was talking to Jesus. But Jesus of Nazareth had been a Jew, and the Jewish people were condemned. Now, why would the Son of the eternal God have to be a Jew if those people were so bad? Didn't it show poor judgment on God's part? Wouldn't an all-knowing God have seen that it was a mistake? And could a modern Nazi student still pray to that Jew, Jesus, without violating our code of living?

I lost weight. Food was not plentiful, and we lived on rations. But even those small meals did not taste good to me and I frequently gave part of my food to my hungry roommate. I could often feel the blue, searching eyes of my favourite teacher rest on me, but I dared not meet them.

One afternoon, having a few minutes free time, I walked quickly to my favourite spot. As I approached the bench, I saw my teacher friend sitting there. Her face had become more serious lately, and her smile carried a hidden sadness. We all knew why!

She was engaged to an SS officer. I had seen his picture several times in her room. He was a tall, handsome young man with sparkling eyes, blond, curly hair, and a proud, sophisticated smile. He had been stationed in Prague several months, but now he had left for the front in Russia. Miss Walde was waiting for a letter, and we all waited eagerly with her. She remained as warm and efficient as usual, but behind her self-control and her smiles we knew she carried unshed tears.

I sat down quietly beside her and watched the windswept clouds. She didn't talk. I knew she waited for me to begin.

I turned to her and said haltingly, "Miss Walde, I'd like to ask you an unusual question. I hope you don't mind!"

She nodded, so I continued. "Do you think that a German youth can be a good Nazi and still pray as folks did in the olden days?"

"Maria Anne," she answered, "I appreciate your question. It shows me that you have a deep longing to do right. But there are two ways for us. The old way is the way of our parents, who live by their old-fashioned knowledge and will live by it until they die. But Hitler has been called by providence to show us young people a better and more scientific way. German youth have a calling, a task to do, for the Supreme Being and Hitler."

Miss Walde spoke persuasively. She shared her deep convictions. I knew she believed what she said.

Well, if she believed in the new religion, it was good enough for me. Yes, she believed in God, too, only a different God, without the stain of Judaism.

"But what about prayer?" I asked.

She smiled again, and promised to give me a little book to read. It would explain everything, she said.

The book, *Wanderer Between Two Worlds,* contained the life story of a well-known Nazi writer. That evening I began to read it. From the beginning his style fascinated me, and I could hardly stop reading to take part in the evening activities.

His chapter on prayer impressed me most. As a growing boy, the writer decided to put God to a test. Taught by his mother to pray for protection, he boldly decided one morning not to pray, to see what would happen. As expected, the day went by without tragedy, and the next day. After a few days he dispensed with prayer for good. Then the author challenged the reader to try the same experiment and see what would become of old-fashioned childish prayer.

I tried it the next day, and it worked! I tried it the second day. Nothing happened. The book must be right. I was big and strong enough to take care of myself. That suited my independent spirit just fine. Dejection left me.

The only thing that bothered me was the thought of Mother. I could still see her at the train station with pleading eyes and hear her say, *"Marichen,* don't forget Jesus."

Mother would never understand my new way of life; she was set in her old beliefs. I didn't worry about Father. I had never cared for his concept of religion anyway. He served a different God than Mother did, and his zealous fanaticism had never left any room for love or communication with his own family and had just made me rebellious. I didn't want to let Mother down, but we had a new world in the making, a new ideology for young people, and the older people with their old-fashioned ways had to be left behind.

I read that book over and over again. I kept it beside my bed and memorized whole paragraphs. I lent the book to other young people and quoted its statements in letters to my friends. The book had shown me a new way of life. It meant victory, honour, fame, national pride. My last reserve had fallen. I had changed gods. I laid my burning heart and life upon the altar of my country—for Hitler.

At that time I heard one of Hitler's speeches over the radio. We listened to all of them, but that address was something special, given at one of the annual sport festivals for the Hitler youth. How that deep voice could send chills down my back!

"Hitler Youth, you are my youth," he said affectionately at the end. 'I believe in you and I claim you, for you are the Germany of tomorrow, *my* Germany of tomorrow."

Thousands of voices drowned out the rest of his words. Young voices responded the way we all felt. *"Heil! Heil! Sieg*

*Heil! Sieg Heil! Heil Hitler!"* We could imagine the sea of out-stretched arms, the eager faces, the exultant shouts. Tears ran down my cheeks as we heard the national anthem over the radio we all stood with outstretched arms to join in, but I was too choked up to sing.

Yes, we all belonged to Hitler, even little me. For the first time in my life I felt someone claimed me as his own—and I *wanted* to belong to him.

Later that evening I went to Miss Walde again.

"Teacher, why did the Fuhrer never get married?"

She gave me a strange look, hesitated for a moment and then said with a gay smile. "The Fuhrer belongs to all of us, Maria Anne; he could never choose one of us above everyone else, or would that seem right to you?"

I shook my head. It made perfect sense to me that the great and wise Fuhrer would feel like that. Yes, we all loved Hitler. He belonged to us and we to him. And if I had to make the supreme sacrifice someday and lay my life down for him, I would be willing to do so. Hitler's war raged and his youth stood ready to die! Fuhrer, command; we obey. Heil Hitler!

# 3
## Could It Be Love?

As war raged on for three years, the difficulties and perplexities of life intensified. We had all expected final victory much sooner than this, and sometimes I wondered why it took our soldiers so long to finish up. I knew that it was only a question of time until Germany and my Fuhrer would win the war; then we could go on with our Nazi programme, teaching the nations our new and better way of life and building a world where peace and brotherhood would reign forever—or at least for the thousand-year Reich that Hitler was planning.

I trusted Hitler and my teachers with the simple credulity of a young girl who had stepped out of her small, innocent world and her hayloft into a new, strange life. But sometimes it seemed so hard to put all the pieces together. Even Hitler's book, *Mein Kampf*, had puzzles for me—so many great words and strange ideas I had never heard before. I couldn't understand many things in the Nazi books I read, but I felt content to trust. Someday I would be grown up and wise like the Fuhrer, I thought, and everything would fall into place. Until then, all I had to do was obey and do my best, though it seemed more and more difficult to do so.

We had never dreamed that the war would bring such hardships. Food became so scarce that I almost forgot how it felt to
be "full" after a meal. Sometimes after dinner my classmates
and I would go down to the kitchen to beg for an additional
piece of black bread, but the Czech cook would throw her
hands up in despair and wail in her broken German, "If I give
you bread now, I shall not have enough for supper. Then you
will have growling stomachs during the night. Oh, you poor
girls! You need more food. You are growing teenagers and
your stomachs have no bottom anyway. Oh, what shall I do
with you?"

We would turn around and smile. Disappointed, hungry
smiles, sure, but what did it really matter to feel a bit hungry
if it was for Germany's great future? We would walk back to
class singing—singing one of our beloved marching songs that
told of victory and of flags waving in the wind.

Duties pressed after classes. I spent many evening hours at
the railway station—the same huge station where I had arrived short years before as a scared, skinny, self-conscious
girl. Now I wore a uniform. Coloured strings in my tie marked
me as a Hitler Youth leader of rank, and with self-confidence I
didn't hesitate to give orders to Czech people when necessary.
As refugees flooded in from the East in ever increasing numbers
we handed out bits of food to the women, children, and elderly
people, hour after weary hour. We comforted the frightened,
gave first aid to the sick, and helped in any way we could,
though forever handicapped by the meagre food and medica-
tion supplies and interrupted by screaming air raid sirens and
other war routine.

I loved to do military hospital duty. We visited wounded
soldiers, took wheelchair patients for walks, or dated blind
soldiers and went with them to the park or to the movies. One
of my favourites was a dark-haired, tall fellow named Erwin.
A grenade had exploded in his face and robbed him forever

of his eyesight and handsomeness. His delight when I took him to a movie made me forget my own weariness. I watched his upturned young face in the darkness as he listened eagerly to all the sounds of the movie while I whispered to him the descriptions of the pictures he could not see. After the movie I took his hand to lead him back to the military hospital. "Little Hansi," he said quietly, "do you know how much I want to see you?"

A big lump formed in my throat. "Yes, Erwin," I said; "I wish so much that you could see—not only me, but everything ... the city, the stars, the river ... everything!"

"I wonder why I had to lose my eyes," Erwin continued. "I wouldn't mind so much to be without arms or legs, but my eyes—it's so dark and lonely where I am!"

I fought tears and couldn't let him know; I had to be brave and give courage.

"Erwin," I said, and I knew I was only adding to the problem, "I don't know why your eyes are gone; I don't know why other soldiers are in wheelchairs; it is all so hard to understand. Most of all, I cannot understand why the other countries hate us Germans so much that they have to start a war with us. Why is everybody trying to destroy our new Reich? All we want is space to live. Hitler says it is because we are the master race and they are all jealous. But why, Erwin, why?"

Erwin grimaced. "I lost my chance to be one of the master race, Hansi; I am a wreck, and would be better off if the grenade had killed me."

I squeezed his hand and my tears began to roll. "Erwin," I said warmly, "remember that the individual is nothing and the Reich must be first. We might not understand everything, but there has to be a deep meaning to it. Someday we will understand."

"I was once as idealistic as you are, little girl," Erwin said hoarsely, "but your ideals get lost when you grope like an idiot

3

from bed to bed, and try to get the food from the plate to your mouth. All I know is that my life is messed up and I can't find any reasons good enough to help me accept my tough luck."

I had no answer. I held his hand, and before I left him I kissed him gently. My mind refused to let his words influence my devotion and loyalty to our great German cause. Though my thinking sometimes became blurred after accumulated hours of uneasy sleep, days of struggle to fit studies with volunteer service, and cold hours in the air raid shelter, I had confidence that the Fuhrer knew what he was doing. His frequent speeches never ceased to inspire me. The war would soon end in certain victory.

Erwin and I never saw each other after that. I had to leave Prague for several weeks to do some student teaching at the city where my sister lived. We knew each other very casually, but there at her urging I went to meet my real father for the first time. It was almost boring to me: we shook hands like polite strangers, and we both acted defensive.

"So, you are a Hitler Youth," Papa said with a thin smile. "I never dreamed that one of my daughters would bring me such honour!" He sounded sarcastic, and we both knew it.

"I am not your daughter, sir," I said icily. "And what I do with my life is none of your concern since you never worried about me when I was a child and needed you."

He opened his mouth and his face reddened, but then he closed his lips tightly and turned away.

I shrugged my shoulders. What was it to me? I belonged to a movement and to my Fuhrer—he didn't. I wouldn't even shake hands with his second wife, a Czech peasant woman. I was ashamed to claim either of them.

I couldn't wait to get back to Prague. My school was my home where I was accepted and secure. How much I loved it!

The highlight of each school day was the arrival of the mailman. Mail was the only thing that was plentiful besides duties.

I liked letters and I enjoyed writing. I would write in the bomb shelter at night, during class recess, and whenever I could find an unoccupied minute. Almost daily I received a handful of mail from friends, including soldiers and officers. We knew how our boys waited for messages from home, and we all tried our best not to make them wait.

Mail did not always bring sunshine. Often it brought heartache. Sometimes a letter addressed to a soldier would be returned to the sender stamped, *"Gefallen für Führer und Vaterland"* (Died for the Fuhrer and fatherland). How those few words under the name of the soldier would blow out the light in our hearts and eyes! Many of these boys had worked together with me in the Hitler Youth organization, and when they had left for military training and the fighting front, I had promised to write faithfully. I had kept my promises to all of them.

The first of my letters to be returned was to Fluntl, a friend of my early teens. A tall blond, he had joined the SS troops. I had liked and admired him for his striking smile, frank blue eyes, bubbling enthusiasm, and sincerity.

For weeks I couldn't believe he was dead. I didn't cry; a Nazi youth was not supposed to cry, for it was the highest realization and greatest honour to die for our cause. I knew that Fluntl had believed in his calling and most likely had died with a heil for the Fuhrer on his lips. Self-sacrifice was the greatest goal for any human being! Would tears not degrade his noble death? I controlled my tears, but I could not control the numbness in my soul. Why did he have to die?

The same question haunted me more deeply a few months later when I took part in a training session at the Nazi welfare headquarters in Reichenberg. My sister Margret and I had corresponded after we visited each other during my student teaching, and I had accepted her invitation to stay with her during that summer. We wanted to know each other better though we didn't seem to have much in common.

One sunny afternoon Papa stepped into the house. I rose to leave since he and I avoided each other by wordless agreement. He waved me back. His face looked ashen and very old.

"Margret." He almost whispered it. "Margret, my girl, you must be brave for your children's sake!"

My sister's form swayed and her big blue eyes revealed that she knew the message.

"Is he dead?" she said.

Papa nodded. "Sit down, girl, sit down. He has died for our leader!"

He gave me a quick look and bit his lips. I got up and left the room. I knew that Papa didn't belong to the Nazi Party, and I had the impression he wanted to say something nasty. But why? It wasn't Hitler's fault that Margret's husband had to die at the Russian front. But whose fault was it? All that dying made no sense, not even for those who were left behind. Margret had two stepchildren and a little baby of her own to care for. The father *couldn't* be dead, but he was!

Margret, however, was better off than many others. Sometimes letters would come back to loved ones with those fateful words: *"Vermisst an der Russischen Kampffront"* (Missing at the Russian front). We dreaded this more than the death note, for it spelled uncertainty, imprisonment, perhaps Siberia. It kept the people in the homeland in mental agony for years, hoping that in some way the missing boy might survive and return home.

Mail helped to keep the war going. As everybody knew, headquarters had ordered that in case of emergency, mail must be delivered even if food must be left behind. The boys could stand hunger as long as they had mail. And it worked both ways. How much easier it was for us to forget the meagre lunch, the aching stomach, the dizziness from missing sleep, when we had interesting letters to read.

One sunny spring day in 1942 I slipped out of class to receive my mail. Among other letters I noticed a long, dignified, white envelope with strange handwriting on it. And what handwriting! Handwriting had been of special interest to me ever since I had read an old book on graphology in the school library. That bold, large script fascinated me, but there was one small problem. The writing was partially so illegible that I couldn't make out the name of the sender. I checked the address again. Yes, the letter was addressed to me—so I tore the envelope open and began to read. Then I sat down with an amused smile and called for my friend Liese to come and see.

Well, who would have thought of that! Several months earlier Liese and I had written letters addressed to an Unnamed Soldier. Someone at Hitler's headquarters had started a campaign for more letter writing from the *Heimatfront* (home line) to the *Kampfront* (fighting front), and had suggested the writing to unknown soldiers. Since mail to the fighting forces had to be marked "*Feldpost*" and did not require postage, the idea had caught fire. Almost everybody was writing to at least one unknown soldier.

Since I liked the looks of our dark-blue-and-gold Navy uniforms best, and none of my friends had ever joined the Navy (the normal choice for most of them was the SS), I had marked my dainty little letter: "To an unknown sailor of the German navy." As we wrote on that rainy autumn day we imagined our unknown servicemen to be handsome, dashing heroes. We dropped our letters into the mailbox, laughing gaily with the excitement of the idea.

Nothing came of the letters, just as we had expected, and soon we dismissed the incident from our minds. From the beginning we had felt uneasy over it, anyway. It seemed strange to write a letter to a man without being asked by him. This didn't fit into our concept of etiquette or our strict code of proud womanhood.

Six months later I held the answer to my forgotten letter in my hand, and my curious classmates kindly offered to help me decipher anything I couldn't read.

I liked the style and vocabulary of the letter; the writer, whose name was Rudy, sounded friendly, polished, and very intelligent, and I was impressed. The letter came from a Navy officer's training school, and the young man sounded busy and ambitious. I answered the same day and he replied promptly.

From letter to letter Rudy began to occupy a more special place in my heart, although I was not willing to admit it even to myself. His big handwriting demanded a lot of stationery and his letters soon became known to our mailman and to our matron for their bulkiness. As the letters came more and more frequently, my friends teased me about it, and that made me furious. How ridiculous! Why couldn't I have a perfectly innocent, platonic correspondence with a nice young Navy officer who seemed to have common interests and ideals similar to mine, without being accused of starting a love affair? Love affair with what? A box of letters, a picture, and a few books he sent to me?

His picture told me that he had dark, soft eyes, and a very warm smile. But I had no idea how his voice sounded, how tall he was, or how he walked or laughed. I didn't know enough about him to like or dislike him. Or did I? After all, wasn't I writing to many dear friends whom I cared about deeply?

In the autumn of that year I received a telegram from Walter, a Marine who had been my close friend for quite a while. My letters to Walter had helped him through happy and lonely hours as a soldier and countless love affairs in past years. His telegram asked me to come at once to see him before he went back to the Russian front. I knew that as a Marine officer he would be sent to the forefront of the most critical battles.

Heavy-hearted, I handed the telegram to the *führerin* (lady director) of the school.

"You may go, Maria," she said kindly. "I wouldn't let everybody go, but I trust you."

My eyes burned and I felt the blood rush to my face. "You *can* trust me," I said. "Walter and I are friends, but I am not his girlfriend—and I am puzzled about this telegram!"

Walter looked serious and withdrawn when he shook my hand to welcome me at the military station in Poland. We made small talk and I checked into a guest house put aside by the army for family members of officers.

The school had given me food-ration stamps for three days. We went into a restaurant to eat. We talked about his reassignment to the Russian front, and I let him know how deeply concerned I felt. He had just recuperated from bullet wounds in his shoulder, and did not look strong enough to face the oncoming Russian winter.

"I would like to be engaged before I leave for Russia," Walter said right out of the blue.

It took me by surprise. "You, Walter, becoming serious with a girl? Well, I never thought I would see the day when you would settle down! Who is the lucky girl?"

"Maybe it's you, Maria Anne. Will you marry me?"

I stared into his open, handsome face and those big, kind eyes which had turned dark blue with deep emotion. Slowly I shook my head and watched his face turn red and dejected.

"Why not, Maria Anne? Would it be so hard for you to love me?"

My eyes studied the handsome figure across the table, from the blond, wavy hair to the broad shoulders decked with the stars and gold of his gala uniform to the big, strong hands which reached over to take my hands.

No, it wouldn't be hard to love that good-looking boy with that deep, masculine voice. As a matter of fact, he was the personified dream of my teen years. He looked so German and strong and prince-charming. He was everything I ever wanted.

"Walter," I said warmly, "it would be easy for me to fall in love with you, but I don't think it would work. You come from a long-established, officers' family with the best German pedigree and tradition. Your family expects you to marry within your own social circles. You keep forgetting that I am an orphan girl with peasant background, and your parents would reject me."

"Nonsense, *Liebling*," Walter retorted. "You know that Hitler has resolved the problem of social caste in our country. As long as you are *Arisch* (not a Jew) and qualified to have healthy children, you are my equal."

I felt my face reddening and I shook my head again. "Walter, I belong to the Hitler movement. They have given me education, status, and home. I can't just drop everything and suddenly become a little housewife, even for someone like you. That wouldn't be fair to the Fuhrer!"

Walter looked straight into my eyes. "Maria Anne, be honest with me. Your reasons don't sound convincing. Do you love someone else?"

I shook my head vigorously.

"What about that Navy man you correspond with? You mentioned him in your letters several times."

I felt the blood rush to my face again. Walter had a vexed smile.

"Listen, little girl," he said. "There has been a change in your letters to me since you started to write to him. Please, be honest with me!"

I shrugged my shoulders in helpless embarrassment. "Walter, there is nothing to tell, honestly. I don't know him. We have never met. I like his letters very much, but you should know me well enough by now—I don't let myself fall in love easily. I only know that I have to meet that boy some day before I can give my heart to anybody or I will go through the rest of my life wondering if I missed out on something. Will you give me time?"

I left that same night on the train. Before I climbed into the crowded railway carriage, Walter took me into his arms and kissed me for the first time.

"*Auf Wiedersehen,* my dear, precious friend," he said in a low voice. "I wish you all the luck in the world; you deserve it. And tell that Navy man to make you happy."

Tears blinded my eyes. I wanted to protest, but I couldn't. Somehow I knew his words were final, though I considered his jealousy about "that Navy man" unfounded. I felt confused and sad. Walter was hurt, and was leaving to face Russian snowstorms, loneliness, and maybe death—and I had added to his hardships.

"I'll write to you every day, Walter," I called as the train pulled away. "You are my best friend!"

Walter turned away without answering.

How much mail from my unknown Navy man really meant to me, I admitted to myself only after we had corresponded for more than a year. All at once the bulky letters stopped. One week, two weeks, three weeks, five weeks passed.

I waited and worried. Would my letter to him come back someday with that dreaded stamp on it—"*Vermisst?*" I feared to ask for my mail. Eagerly I listened to the Navy news during "radio hour" in the evening, especially the U-boat news. Rudy had become a third officer on a submarine that year, and I knew something about the odds against those men.

The girls began to tease me again, in a sympathetic sort of way. They seemed slightly puzzled that I would worry so much about a stranger. I denied my concern too loudly and convinced nobody. I began to reason with myself; was I not being absurd to have that man so much on my mind? Maybe he cared nothing about me. Or did he care as much as I did? Why did he write such long letters so often?

Maybe his boat was lost. Maybe he had just decided to stop writing. No, deep inside I knew that my young officer was not dead. He couldn't be. I had to meet him someday, somewhere. He had become part of my life. I had to believe in him and his future.

When after long weeks his next letter arrived, the matron waited until after dinner to give it to me. She said she knew I wouldn't have bothered to eat if I had been given my twenty-page letter to read, and I was already too skinny.

I tore the parcel-letter open, struggling to hold back the happy tears and caring nothing for the teasing remarks of my friends. I had a letter to read, and I read it hurriedly the first time, carefully and slowly a second and third time.

Rudy had been out for many weeks. *Feindfahrt* (patrol), they called it when the boats cruised the ocean and hunted convoys. His letter was a diary, and there had been no opportunity to mail it for many weeks. Certain things they were forbidden to mention, but whatever was permissible he told. I didn't care how many ships they had torpedoed or where his boat had operated; all I wanted to know was about him personally. In one part of his letter he wrote, "When I stand on the bridge during the long hours of my night watch, I look up and see the stars, and I wonder, Maria Anne, if you are asleep or if you are looking at the same stars. Someday, my dear pen pal, we are going to meet each other, and I cannot wait to see you."

That night I looked at his picture for a long, long time. I knew every line of his face by heart, but I had to study it anew.

After I had put the picture down and turned out the lights, I slipped quietly to the window behind my bed and lifted the tight shades a few centimetres. I knew it was against the rules, for every house in the country had to be darkened at night; any beam of light could betray human dwellings to the bombers, which found their targets anyway with deadly precision night after night. Nobody in his right mind ever lifted a shade before morning dawn—but I had to! I had to see the stars just once in a while, for they had been my friends since earliest childhood. I had watched those wandering lights from my bed in the hayloft many a night and had talked with them in my heart.

Now the time had come to talk to the stars again. I had greetings to send! Somewhere a small U-boat sailed on a wide ocean. On it stood a young navy officer with brown eyes and a high, intelligent forehead. He might look up at the stars tonight. Would the stars take my greeting to him? Would the stars tell him of the shy love in my heart and the dreams I couldn't help dreaming? Never would I dare to put my feelings into words. Our friendship seemed so precious and frail that words could have destroyed the beauty of it.

When I let the shades down and slipped under my coarse blanket, Micherle, the girl in the next bed to me, begged, "Sing us to sleep again, Hansi, please."

As so often before, I sang for the girls gladly. They relaxed and so did I. All the melancholy hits I had learned from the radio I sang softly into the darkness—the sad words of love and loneliness and war that tore hearts apart, and while I sensed some of the longing tears that were shed in some beds I finished with my favourite song: "I know that someday something wondrous will happen and I *know* that we shall meet again—" When, Rudy? When will we meet?

# 4
# Prince Charming at the Door

As total war raged in the summer of 1944, we girls were shipped out of the city into the Sudeten mountains. Germany had forgotten what vacation meant; so had we. At nineteen, I became leader of a group of girls engaged in hard farm labour. Our male farm hands had gone to the fighting fronts. Desperately the women planted and hoed and harvested, learning to do men's work and do it very fast.

Our arms ached as we raked and pulled and lifted from early morning to late afternoon. But we all understood. The farm wife where I worked was sweet and motherly, but she looked haggard and overworked. Each day she slipped some extra food into my apron pocket. I tried to return my appreciation in diligent labour. We became the best of friends.

The extra food, the summer sun, and the large amount of exercise in the fresh air did me many favours. No longer so bony, I also acquired a healthy tan. My hair, worn in a pageboy style, had grown long over my shoulders, and the sun had bleached it almost blonde. War seemed far away in our out-of-the-way camp. No air raids disturbed us as we slept in the quietness of the whispering evergreen woods. Every morning the singing birds awakened us. The morning dew glistened like a thousand diamonds over the pastures when we marched out to the villages for work. When we stood around the flagpole to salute, our voices shouted the pledge with vigour. This was the best summer for me since my childhood—and Rudy still wrote long letters regularly.

Late one afternoon we checked in from the village, took ice-cold showers, and prepared for supper and evening training. Most of the girls gathered at the athletic field around a girl with an accordion for square dancing and happy chatter. My duties as a subleader made me late, but I hummed a tune while brushing my hair and creaming my sunburned arms. Then I fell to musing again. I hadn't heard from Rudy for a while and I tried hard not to worry. It was disgusting that I couldn't get that boy out of my head!

It was almost time to leave for the city again. Soon we would have to pack and return to Prague. How I hated to leave! The summer had been so peaceful. Sure, there had been some friction with that *Führerin*. She was the assistant camp director, and she and I had not been able to get along; but outside of that it had been a dream of a summer. The only thing missing to make everything perfect would have been a visit from—well, no sense wishing again. Rudy would never be able to come to this remote place. Why should he, anyway?

Starting down the stairway opposite the entrance, I whistled a tune and threw back my long hair, resolutely tossing my head to indicate my determination to stop my silly dreaming.

All at once I stopped short. Through the high, sunflooded open door stepped a Navy officer. His face looked very familiar. Yes, I knew every line of that face by heart—and I wondered if I were dreaming! Then I panicked and fled back up to my quarters. With shaking knees I sat on the edge of my cot and tried to control my beating heart and racing thoughts. I didn't know a girl could feel so terribly scared and so happy all at once. Oh dear, what if he didn't like my looks? What if—I began to brush my long hair again, reset my service pin on my blue house uniform, check myself for invisible spots and blemishes, and wish with all my heart that fairy tales could be true and I would turn into a beautiful princess—but I didn't!

Presently I heard my name being called. Summoning all the courage I could find, I walked slowly down the stairs and reported respectfully to the leader in charge. With an amused twinkle in her eyes, she pointed at the Navy man and said, "You have a visitor, Maria Anne. Come and welcome him!"

I looked full into his smiling face and extended my hand to him. Rudy smiled broadly and said, just a shade too lightly, "Well, here I am, little Hansi!"

I nodded and managed to stammer, "Yes, I can see it—" I could feel myself blushing.

Since my superior had never seen me speechless or self-conscious before she first looked puzzled and then she laughed a hearty laugh. That broke the tension in the room. Rudy and I also began to laugh, and I finally managed enough self-composure to welcome him and invite him to join the group outside under the big tree, where everybody square danced.

Suddenly aware of the sensation Rudy's appearance created, I got my self-confidence back quickly. Proudly I introduced him to my friends; behind his back they gave me little signs of approval or envy. I beamed with delight.

When the supper bell called, Rudy was invited to dine with us. He was seated beside the camp director, a woman of high leadership rank and strict manners. I fulfilled my supervising duties, but I couldn't stop my heart from beating loudly, especially when I stole glances across at Rudy's place. A born charmer, he carried on a gallant conversation with the lady of the camp and at the same time he watched me closely with, it seemed to me, a look of slight amusement. By the end of the meal the *Führerin* of the camp was so favourably impressed by his gentlemanly behaviour that she had me signed off from further duty for the evening and the next day, even before I dared ask. Since she had never done such a thing before, this created an even bigger sensation among the girls.

After I had changed into my uniform and returned, we walked slowly out, aware that many eyes watched us. Once outside the campus we turned towards the sunset. We walked in an enchanted world, glowing with golden-red and purple. A strange silence hung between us as Rudy took my hand to help me up the hill. We stood there for a long time watching the fading colours of the evening sky.

We had both felt so close to each other in our letters. Though we had never mentioned this in words, our deep feeling showed between the lines of every page. Now we recognized that the hour of testing of our friendship had come. Both of us feared that one wrong word, one untrue gesture, could break the tender thread. Our friendship now had to face reality. I did not look up as I felt Rudy's eyes searching my profile. Slowly the golden twilight turned into velvety darkness.

"Are you disappointed, little Hansi?" Rudy asked gently.

I shook my head too vigorously and quickly replied: "No— are you, Rudy?"

He denied it too, but we both knew we lied. Yes, we both felt disappointed. Not that either of us didn't like the other; we were just different from what the other expected. Dreams are perfect; humans never are. Two and a half years of unreal friendship had suddenly come to an end, and our dreams were irretrievably gone. Would our ties prove strong enough to face reality and go on?

We were determined to give it a try. Sitting on a log, we began to talk. I had so many questions to ask, and I sat and listened as he told me about his life.

He was the only son of a well-to-do, long-established family in a German village in the province of Silesia. His only sister was two years younger than Rudy. His father owned the best

*Gasthaus* (inn) and a meat business. Rudy had never experienced poverty or want.

He had been the idol of his grandmother, who lived in the same house. The maid of the house, faithful old Selma, called him "Prince" and treated him as such.

"I must have been a typical 'spoiled' boy," Rudy mused, "and I sometimes wished I had not got away with as much as I did—but Grandma never denied me a wish and even now my parents may grumble but I get whatever I desire."

As Rudy reminisced about his childhood, I could picture that cute, small fellow so easily—a boy living in his lone dream world amidst all the attention and fuss three women showered upon him, trying hard to be tough and excelling in all the boys' activities of the village, especially in sports. He coasted through school, succeeding without trying. During his teen years he attended the *Gymnasium* (secondary school) in the province's capital of Breslau. There he had too much freedom and money on his hands. Then the war!

"I volunteered to the Navy after the *Abitur* (final secondary school examination), and my grandfather said I wouldn't be able to stand the hardships. I told him that on my first leave home after basic training I would return either with the rank of officer, or with the Iron Cross!"

"Did you return with one of the two?" I asked eagerly.

"I had both, my rank and the medal." Rudy sounded pleased and proud in a nonchalant way, though his voiced stayed soft.

"Rudy, how did you get your medal?"

Silence deepened a while before he answered.

"I don't like to think about it," he said at last. "It was after I had begun my duty as a machine gunner on a patrol boat. We were guarding convoys. One particular day we escorted a big convoy through the Straits of Calais. About twenty Spitfires and as many bombers attacked us."

"What are Spitfires?"

Rudy laughed. "I am sorry that I expect so much war knowledge from you, little Hansi. Spitfires are Engilsh fighter planes. And it is those Spitfires which the patrol boats have to reckon with. The bombers always concentrate on the convoy, but the fighter planes try to wipe out the anti-aircrafts on the patrol boats. Those planes have a rather unique way of diving down at the boats." Rudy kept his voice casual. "They first shoot into the water, and the bullets splash a little path toward the boat. Then, when they have a good aim, they really let you have it."

I shivered, and Rudy moved protectively closer to me. Silence hung again.

"Rudy, how did you get the medal?"

"Well, I shot down two Spitfires that day, and did a few other small things."

"Like—?"

"Oh, the two men who handed me the ammunition were knocked out after the attack and I noticed our boat still was running in big circles. We did that so we wouldn't be a steady aim for the fighter planes. So I got out of the straps of my anti-aircraft gun and looked around and the deck was a mess. It finally dawned on me that something must be wrong up at the bridge. I raced up and everybody was either dead or disabled. The rudder man was dead and had slumped into the helm. I took his body out and turned the rudder wheel to midships. Then I gave orders to stop the engines. At that time I wasn't able to run a whole ship."

"I am glad that you are now with the U-boats," I said, relieved. "That isn't so dangerous for you because you are under water."

Rudy laughed again. "That's how little girls picture U-boat war, don't they! U-boats are very seldom under water, little Hansi. We submerge only when we attack by day or when we are attacked. By night we try to get away on the surface even when we are chased. We can move faster."

4

"Are you often chased?" I tried to sound casual.

"Well, things were not too bad until 1943. We definitely had the upper hand in the Atlantic Ocean."

"Did it turn bad after America entered the war? I always wondered why they had to in the first place. We never did anything to them."

"No, it wasn't that. We could sink their boats faster than the United States and England could build them. Our problem began with something we couldn't put our fingers on for a while. The English call it radar. It was the most spooky thing when it all began. We were so used to relaxing during the night, nearly always operating on the surface, even when we wolf-packed enemy convoys. It is next to impossible to see a little U-boat in the darkness of the night, so we never paid much attention to enemy planes except during the daytime. Then one night the floodlight of an enemy fighter plane caught us, and we couldn't shake the light by zig-zagging."

"Why didn't you submerge?"

"We finally did, but we knew that we were a dead duck. Very often a U-boat cannot submerge to a safe depth as fast as a fighter plane can come around on a second run and dump all its depth charges on us. Luckily they missed us!"

"Why did they find you in the first place?"

"We had no idea for months, and those weeks were living hell for all German U-boats and Admiral Doenitz. We lost so many boats—" Rudy's voice turned very low and he reached for my hand. ". . . So many of my best friends died—I sometimes wonder why I got through all of it without a scratch. Some of thoses who died right beside me were so much better and nobler than I am. I do so many foolish things whenever we come back to the ports."

"What *is* radar?" I interrupted.

"Radar has made our patrols suicide missions," Rudy said tensely. Then he stopped as my hands tightened. I had sent a message—I felt scared! Scared for this beloved stranger who wasn't a stranger and who talked about death so matter-of-factly.

He laughed suddenly. "Little girl, have I come such a long way after such a long time to talk about war to you? Don't worry; *we* know now what radar is and we will soon have means to counteract it. We will soon have different boats. too. They can stay for months under water and I expect to be called on one as a second commander. And the war will soon be over!"

It was good to listen to him. He sounded so young and yet mature. I knew why he had never got hurt during all those years, but I couldn't tell him that. Destiny had brought him safely to me, because I *had* to meet him or my heart would have been empty and wondering forever.

I watched the stars appear above us, one by one, until the night sky became a diamond-sprinkled dome that surrounded us with new assurance. The disappointment had gone; he really was as I had pictured him all along.

And all at once I felt, too, that Rudy had received my greetings all through the past years; for the stars began to talk to us again, and we sat and listened. The stars stepped out of the sky and began to shine within my heart, and I felt that two lights shone in my eyes as we walked hand in hand back to the camp. We both had lost something; our pen pals had left us, but we had found something more precious.

The next day found us happy and at ease with each other. We felt as if we had seen each other many times in the past. I showed him the beautiful countryside, and in high spirits we climbed some hills. Proudly I showed him off to "my" farmers. My motherly friend acted a little shy, but seemed impressed by all the "brass" and medals. She got busy, and in short time she had fixed packed lunches for us. She wouldn't listen to my suggestion to let us both help her with her work before we left. We strolled to my little hideouts around the country where I had sat and written to him and dreamed of the time we would meet.

When I least expected it, Rudy took me into his strong arms to kiss me. I quickly freed myself from his arms and shook my head.

Rudy looked utterly baffled and distressed. Why couldn't he understand? I knew that he had kissed many girls, but he and I—couldn't he understand that it had to be different? For years we had treasured our friendship as something very special. Would it have to go as most war affairs did—passion, kisses, jokes, fights, leaving a bitter taste in the mouth when it was over? Never! I couldn't fall in love, fall out, and fall in again as some girls do. Maybe I was a dreamer, but I believed someday there would be a great love in my life. I couldn't possibly end this unusual friendship with Rudy in any cheap way, or as an everyday love affair.

Rudy listened seriously to my attempt to explain how I felt. Then, lifting my chin gently till I looked right into his eyes, he said, "Maria Anne, have I given you any reason to believe that I would like to use you in any cheap way, or for a fleeting love affair? You have become a part of my life, my great inspiration! I cannot picture my life without you and your letters any more. You are the type of girl I want to marry someday. Would you?"

Had I heard right? He hadn't by any chance proposed to me? How could he? We had met each other just the day before. I buried my face on his shoulder and as his arms gently enfolded me I looked up. His eyes assured me that my heart had found the great love of my life. Yes, my heart had found its home and his lips found mine.

Later as we sat in the sun, he talked to me about our future together. Suddenly he said, "My little Hansi, here I am talking to you about our future home, and I am just realizing that I know hardly anything about you. All we do is talk about me and my life; tell me about yourself, your childhood, your family—"

I shrugged my shoulders. What could I tell him? About the little house by the woods, and about my hayloft? Would he understand? He had grown up so differently; he had financial security and the luxuries of life even during the war. Could I tell him of the time when Mother stood at the train station worrying because I might forget God? How could he ever understand? He had a nominal Protestant background, but religion meant nothing to him. He was a Nazi, like me; and he trusted in Hitler and the future of the Reich. What was there to tell?

'Rudy, there isn't much to tell about me. I am just an orphan girl brought up in a very religious foster home. My foster-father was a bricklayer, my real papa a gardener. I am poorer than a mouse and just lucky enough that I was selected by the Germans after our occupation to be educated in Prague. You know that I am a youth leader and I plan to advance." I took a deep breath because memories hit me.

"I never thought much about marriage because it would interfere with my future plans. I have wondered before—" my memory saw myself sitting across a table from a distressed blond officer saying the same words, and I felt a sharp pain. "Wouldn't I let everybody down if I got married? I must serve the Fuhrer and Germany someday in a special way to repay all the free education I am getting."

"I have a better idea," Rudy grinned. "Why couldn't we do those things together? As soon as the war is over I plan to go into the Merchant Marine, and I will often be gone. You can fufill your calling and teach. I will not demand all your time."

I smiled, relieved. How simple everything was; how great and how simple! The time had come to stop worrying and let go. The great moment of my young life had arrived. I had found my love, and I could trust myself in his hands. Rudy was intelligent, mature, and wise. He had the answers to all my problems, and I was an ignorant little girl who wouldn't stop worrying.

But now I knew somebody loved me, and for the first time I dared to love back. War, torpedoes, bombs, death—all seemed impossible as we sat close to each other in the flowering pasture with grazing cows on one side and stately evergreens on the other. Above us fluffy white clouds drifted in the bright summer sky over the hazy mountains. Maybe I was dreaming and would wake up to find everything gone and grey, but I would enjoy the dream while it lasted. With new confidence I looked into Rudy's face. Then I looked at the golden band he had put on my finger. At the wedding our rings would be moved from the left hand to the right.

The next day we travelled together to Rudy's home. We didn't feel quite as carefree as we had the day before. Rudy was obviously nervous and I dreaded facing his family. We made small talk and laughed about our funny remarks, but we both knew that we were two scared young people who might be heading into opposition.

Rudy's parents, his sister, and the maid stood in the doorway to welcome us, and in spite of my awkward shyness I couldn't help feeling amused when I noticed how Rudy hid his left hand behind his back. So did I, for neither of us had taken our golden bands off before our arrival.

Rudy's mother was a short woman, but stately, with silver-streaked hair and restless brown eyes. "We welcome you to our home," she said with a polite smile. Her eyes did not smile with her, but examined me coolly while we shook hands.

Rudy's father, a very short but heavy man with watery blue eyes, pulled me down to kiss me on my cheek. His red nose spoke of a liking for liquor and he wheezed with each breath. Rudy had told me of his father's weak heart, and now I worried more than ever; how would Rudy announce our quick engagement without hurting anyone?

"Maria Anne and I are engaged," Rudy said casually and we both brought our left hands forward—I with the intention of grabbing his right hand because all at once my knees felt like soft butter and I couldn't breathe.

The smiles froze on their faces, but Annemarie, Rudy's sister, saved the moment and broke the shocked silence.

"I am so happy for both of you," she said warmly, embracing both of us at the same time. "Come in and feel at home. Dinner is waiting!"

We stepped in and Selma, the maid, took our coats. I soon found that Selma was not a hired worker but a long-time friend of the family. She had begun her service as a young girl when she began working for Rudy's grandparents during the early years of their marriage. When Rudy's parents inherited the restaurant and the butcher shop, Selma also came to them. Rudy and his sister were the third generation of that family she had loved and cared for.

"Our prince has brought home a princess," Selma announced proudly to the guests in the homey, dark-panelled guest dining room as we walked through the restaurant to the family dining room. The whole house breathed secure wealth and old-fashioned taste. I saw a carved, dark mahogany table set with china and heavy linen. We sat down to delicious, rich food, well-prepared by Rudy's mother, who never left the cooking to anyone else. Rudy had talked about her gourmet cooking and seemed very proud of it. Her eyes softened a little when I told her that I hadn't eaten so well in years.

Annemarie, who sat to my right, chattered gaily and urged me to eat more than I could. My stomach churned into knots.

I liked Annemarie from the first moment I saw her. Only two years older than I, she acted as if we were already sisters. Her eyes had the same hazel colour as Rudy's. She was about my height, but slimmer, and she reminded me of an expensive china doll I had once admired. She looked so delicate and very special to me.

Annemarie tried her best to make my stay comfortable. She shared her bedroom with me, and I wondered how it would feel to be the only daughter of a wealthy home who had a whole room with heavy oak furniture, ruffly curtains, and a bed canopy to herself. But it was too hard for my imagination.

I felt awkward and uneasy around Rudy's parents. Maybe they felt uneasy too! Our engagement had taken not only his family but the whole village by surprise. However, the "prince" and I spent every moment with each other trying to get fully acquainted; we did not worry or care unduly about anything or anybody else.

How our time flew! We tried to ignore the fact that parting time approached, hoping that by ignoring it we could stop the hour from coming. We had a small engagement party with red roses and fancy wines, which almost scared me in its richness and strangeness. Then Rudy and I rode in a horse-drawn buggy to the train station. The little country train brought us rapidly to Breslau, capital of the privince of Silesia. There our two trains were to leave in opposite directions in the afternoon.

We arrived before noon, and Rudy took the opportunity to show me his beloved city during our few remaining hours together. For seven years he had gone to school in Breslau, and he knew every corner of that picturesque old place. We ate a few bites in a small cafe, paying not only with money but also with ration stamps provided to his mother. At last the moment came when we had to return to the railway terminal. For each other's sake we had put on smiles and made lighthearted conversation, trying to disguise how we felt about parting.

Rudy had to leave first. After checking our suitcases we walked down to the platform and found the train. Rudy's compartment with the first class, reserved for the "better" element of society even during the days of total war. He reserved his place, stored his suitcase away, and stepped down once more from the train. I had determined to be a brave sweetheart up to the minute of his leaving, and I forced a smile. Trying to cheer me up, Rudy took me into his arms. "Don't be sad, my dear Hansi, we shall see each other soon again. Be my brave little girl meanwhile and wait for me. We shall write to each other every day."

That did it! Hiding my face on his shoulder, I burst into uncontrolled sobbing. He pulled out a spotless white handkerchief and began to wipe my face tenderly. I looked up into his kind face and again I felt premonition, that dreadful feeling of danger ahead that I had known when I left my mother to go into Nazi training. Why was I so afraid? I tried to control myself, but it was no use. I cried bitterly, while my heart felt like a stone.

The conductor raised the signal plate and blew the whistle. Rudy kissed me once more and then had to let me go and swing himself onto the already moving train. His face showed the strain of the hour and a deep concern for me. Struggling to calm myself, I finally managed to smile through my tears, but I could not speak. The train gathered speed, and Rudy's waving, navy-blue arm with golden stripes and stars grew smaller and dimmer in the distance.

Even after the train had disappeared, I still waved. Then I stopped waving to wipe my tears and began to search for my own train. How I found it and got on it I couldn't remember later.

Would I ever see him again? Would he come back from war? What lay ahead of us? For a few short days I had experienced the warmth of love, the joy of togetherness, the security of having found a home for my heart. All I could think of was Rudy. All I wanted was to be with him. But the trains rolled on into the evening—mine toward the east, his toward the west. Each minute tore us farther apart, while the sun died and the day turned into a long night.

War waited for him; the big city called for me. I cherished the memory of some wonderful days, and the slim golden ring on my finger. As I lifted my hand to feel his ring on my hot face, the golden metal felt cold and strange, just like my lonely heart.

Train wheels sang again, and this is what they sang: "*Ich liebe Dich; auf Wiedersehen. Ich liebe Dich—*" (I love you; good-bye. I love you—).

Beloved sailor, good-bye.

# 5
# Spectre of Death

I held Rudy's letter in my hand. "My beloved little bride,"
he wrote. "It is just like a dream that you and I finally met.
Remember that I love you and that we have a long life before
us to get better and better acquainted. Wait for me and don't
be lonely, for my heart is always with you until I come back and
take you in my arms never to let you go again . . . with many
kisses . . ."

Tears streamed again. It wasn't only that I missed him
terribly; I felt utterly confused and scared. Everything seemed
so easy and simple while we were together. It had also been easy
to write to him as an unknown serviceman for so long. But I
didn't feel prepared to answer love letters; I didn't know how!

Of course Rudy could write those with ease, and so affectionately. He wrote nearly every day. Still I could not shake a nagging fear that this was all an unreal dream. Sometimes I even
found myself wishing we were still on undefined terms, when
I could hide my deep feelings for him safely behind poetry and
profound thoughts.

Rudy came from a home where he had been cuddled, pam-
pered, and loved all his life; I spent my childhood where show
of affection was considered weakness. The only time I had ever

fondled anything was when as a young child I had been given a pet goat one spring. He and I had been inseparable. He often jumped on my back and nibbled my ear. In return I pressed my face into his coarse white baby-fur and squeezed him tight, but only when nobody was looking. Once I even kissed him goodnight, for I had read in a story about families kissing each other in the evening. But Sepp saw me kissing my goat and teased me for weeks. I was mortified.

How does a young peasant girl act when she finds herself engaged to a sophisticated prince charming who is wise in the ways of the world?

My letters changed very little. They were long, sharing my innermost thoughts, but oh, so shy when it came to the expressions of love.

Shortly after our engagement, Rudy celebrated his twenty-second birthday. With small means and much thought, I wrapped my gifts for him. Two books, a little scrapbook filled with my own poems and drawings, candies saved from the dinner table for weeks, and then my letter. It took all my courage but I finally managed to do it. For the first time I ended my letter: "I send you all my love and a kiss, your little Hansi."

Rudy's answer was charming. He thanked me for my gifts and at the very end he tucked in a small P.S. "Little Hansi, do you give kisses only on birthdays? Too bad that birthdays come only once a year!"

I could picture Rudy's amused smile behind the words, and I put my head on his long letter and cried.

I was afraid. Afraid of his demanding love and of myself! Would I make him a good wife? Did I have it in me to make him happy? I was so exhausted; the demands of war and studies seemed to go beyond my strength. And as time went on, I felt a strange note in Rudy's epistles. I asked him what was bothering him, but at first he ignored my questioning.

After three months he told me the truth. His parents, practical and business minded, had disapproved of our unusual romance from the beginning. They tried to discourage Rudy from continuing our relationship, and their arguments had the force of parental authority. Rudy's home was very dear to him, and family disharmony proved highly disturbing to his easy-going nature. At last he could hide his problem no longer and told me about it.

I had no choice. I pulled my golden band from my finger, wrapped it in cotton, and sent it without any written message to his parents. Then came the harder part, to write my last letter to him. This is what I wrote: "Rudy, today I sent my ring back to your mother. There is no question in my mind that I must never stand between you and your parents. I should say, your mother and you. I know how much home means to you, and I know also that you must never give up your home for my sake.

"I do not know why your mother is against me. I realize that you are wealthy and yours is a very respectable family, while I am only an orphan girl. But Rudy, this part of life I couldn't help; it is not my fault. You know I am trying to find my calling. I might be poor, but I can be proud. I have dedicated my life to the Fuhrer and our fatherland, and I shall do my best.

"Rudy, I never did anything wrong to your mother or you. The only thing she may hold against me is that I have trusted you and that I loved you. May you both forgive me for that!

"I do want to thank you for those wonderful days which we spent together. Somehow I knew from the beginning that it was only a dream and someday there would be a rude awakening.

"Rudy, you know me well enough; you will understand that there can never be a coming back for us. I have nothing but my pride to protect me, for I am alone in this world. We must forget each other, and I will do all I can to forget my love for you because my heart has no more right to love. You have been the first and only one I ever trused enough to love, and it might sound bitter when I say that I wish I had not dared to trust you. It is well said that one doesn't know love until one feels love's anguish. But it seems a lot of ache for a few moments of happiness. Maybe I was never meant to love a man. Maybe I must live only for my work. I don't know if I shall ever dare to love somebody again.

"For your future I wish you only the best and much luck! May you come back unharmed from the war to your family, and may your honourable mother find a girl for you that will make her and you happy!

"For the last time I send you my greeting and my love. Farewell! Maria Anne."

My heart swelled with bitter resentment. I felt humiliated and, oh, so lonely! I had not only lost my love—I had lost a sister, too. For Annemarie, Rudy's sister, and I had become best of friends and were corresponding regularly. But as I had feared all along, it all had been a mistake—a pipe dream, a fairy tale with a cruel ending.

I did not cry a single tear. The hurt was too deep, the storm in my proud heart too great, to find relief. I busied myself with my duties and studies, lying awake for long hours waiting for the air-raid sirens to sound. I had no more desire to see the stars, so the shades stayed shut tight. Autumn mornings were chilly, and we felt the coal shortage as we shivered in our classrooms. Frosts browned the last purple flower beds as mother earth prepared for a cold winter sleep. My numb heart followed her example.

It took iron self-control to march out every morning into biting rain to salute the dripping flag. I hadn't felt warm for days; there was no place to get warm. The rooms were damp and clammy. Our food rations were meagre, but it didn't matter to me—I wasn't hungry. One morning I stood before the flagpole saluting when a wave of dizziness overcame me. I forced myself to march back into the house. Then I collapsed.

They put me in a youth hospital in Brünn, a smaller city. We had excellent treatment, but I was too sick to notice or care. "Contagious jaundice infection" was the diagnosis. The epidemic had raged for weeks, and the hospital was overcrowded. Before long I had lost the robustness I had gained in the summer. I grew pale and emaciated. I tried not to think too much, for life seemed a strange puzzle with no answers.

Days turned into weeks. My lady doctor ordered new X-rays for me, which revealed a stomach ulcer. Sitting down at my bedside, the doctor gave me a motherly smile as she asked, "Little Hansi, is there anything that bothers you—any kind of heartache or worry or problem? You are so listless and withdrawn."

"No." I shook my head defiantly and proudly. I wasn't willing to admit even to myself that anyone could throw me off balance. And Rudy was a closed issue.

A few days later, after my eighteenth birthday in November, the nurse brought me a forwarded letter. The envelope revealed Rudy's familiar handwriting, and the return address showed that he had been promoted. *"Oberleutnant zur See,"* it read. I wondered if he had been called to his new position as second commander on one of the newest U-boats, as he had expected. How proud his parents would be! I wondered if my pride would permit me to open his letter. Yes, I tore the envelope eagerly and read. It was an affectionate birthday message. I read it over and over again, especially the sentence, "Little Hansi, I couldn't let your birthday go by without sending you my warmest wishes—"

No, it was no use. I had to be firm. Quickly I folded his letter up, put it into a new envelope, and mailed it back to him. Rudy didn't know I was so sick, and I didn't want him to know.

Slowly I regained strength and finally one afternoon the doctor promised that I could leave the hospital the next day. I rejoiced. That night, which I thought would be my last one in that house of sickness, the air-raid sirens forced us all out of our beds and into the shelter. Huddled in blankets, we listened indifferently to the droning of the enemy bombers. We always asked the same question: Would the bombers pass over us, or would our own place be their target for the night? We found out all too soon. The bombs exploded nearer and nearer. We knew that the bomb that would hit us would come without singing, so we just sat and waited. By far the hardest attack I had ever experienced, it left us tense and terrified.

At last the siren sounded the departure of the airplanes, and we were allowed to climb back up to our rooms and into our beds. But sleep would not come. We had opened our shades to watch the burning city. Gas and electricity were out, and nurses used flickering candles to take care of some very sick youngsters. The night sky was red from fires and dense with smoke. As I looked out at the dreadful scenes of destruction, I thought of the many lives that had been snuffed out. Nagging questions again tortured me.

All at once I noticed some nurses excitedly run to and fro whispering. I slipped out of bed, still numb and cold from hours in the shelter, and joined the nurses.

What was the problem? Somebody, they said, had detected a dark object on the back ramp of the building, which proved to be *Ein Blindgänger*, a bomb that for some reason had not exploded when it hit the ground. Either it was a time bomb that would explode in a matter of minutes or hours, or it was an ordinary bomb with a short circuit in the releasing device. In any case, the bomb was close enough to demolish the small hospital if it exploded, and shatter the windows and sliding doors in our faces.

Since any strong vibration, even a loud scream, could explode the bomb, the patients could not be taken down to the shelter nor could the building be evacuated. There was no place to go, for everything around us was fire and ruins.

Noiselessly I stepped up to the back window. In the glow of burning houses across the river I saw the pear-shaped object in its dark outline. Some others stepped up beside me as the news spread quickly through the ward. The nurses tried to hide the news, fearing panic, but without success. Some patients pulled their blankets over their heads, others cried softly—but everybody tried to avoid commotion and fast movements.

I pressed my hot forehead against the cold window glass. Death and I faced each other again, and my heart started to argue with the grim visitor. I had so many questions to ask, and nobody would answer.

Who was I? Why was I born? Where had I come from and where was I going? If I had to die that night, what could have been the purpose and reason for my existence? Why must "self-sacrifice" be the highest fulfilment for a human being? Everything seemed shallow and intangible in the face of death. My high ideals and goals seemed powerless to comfort. I imagined that the Grim Reaper sat out there on top of that metal object and grinned into my bewildered eyes.

My heart cried out for more understanding and more insight; but smoke covered the fading stars, and the dawn had to fight its way through charred ruins and clouds of dust. Everything within and around me seemed vague and empty. We just stood motionless and waited.

As soon as it was light enough, a noiseless crew appeared. Obviously the men were prisoners, as an armed guard marched behind them. Since we young people had never heard about concentration camps and political prisoners, we had no idea who those sad, grey figures were. They moved in cautiously, like cats, towards the bomb and examined it long and carefully. Then one man bent over while others handed him some tools. Ever so precisely he began to take the detonator apart. At last he stopped, nodded, got up from his knees, and wiped his fore-head. The bomb was *entschärft* (disarmed), and the prisoners carried the different parts away.

Normal life resumed in the ward, and a nurse ordered me back to bed. With a last look out of the window, I turned away. I had seen the Grim Reaper walk out of the yard. Once again he had turned his back on me as he returned to the smouldering city to find more prey among the ruins. But I had a strange foreboding that we would meet again!

After a few days, as soon as a certain amount of order had been established and trains were running again, I was dismissed. I reported back to school at once in spite of my doctor's recommendation to take a vacation and recover my full health. Where should I go to find rest? The little house in the woods was so far away, and I hadn't heard from Mother for a long time. Mail was delayed. Too many trains and tracks were being destroyed. Rudy was not mine any more, and I had no right to go to his comfortable home in eastern Germany. Possibly his parents and sister were not even there any more. I had heard rumours that the Russians had already broken through into Silesia and the refugees had fled through winter storms to get away.

No, I had nowhere to go, and I was eager to work again. My staff leader received me gladly, for every willing hand was needed to meet the emergencies of total war. Week after week we struggled and toiled, often sharing our small food rations with refugees and wounded soldiers who seemed more hungry than we. My stomach gave me terrible pains. Ulcers demanded certain kinds of food, but who cared about such trivialities?

Miss Walde's big blue eyes watched me with increasing concern. She insisted that I would take off every so often and go for a *bummel* (stroll) through the city. It was unheard of in school to be that favoured, but I was so pale and painracked most of the time the other students didn't object.

One sunny spring afternoon I strolled listlessly through the old town square, stopping at a small stand which offered some pale postcards and homemade curiosities for sale. It always astonished me how the Czech people managed to "sell" things out of nothing; for the total war had scraped away everything useable. There was no safety pin, toothbrush, stationery, or any other luxury to be found anywhere. Our shoes were soled with wood and the tops were cloth. My only shoes had holes, my uniform was faded.

In deep thought I rummaged through the postcards, a rarity, trying to find some suitable pictures to send to friends, when a very pleasant low voice made me jump.

*"Mein Fräulein, brauchen sie einen Begleiter?"* (Miss, do you need an escort?)

Annoyed, I looked over my shoulder. I detested street introductions of any kind, but what I saw softened my indignation. There stood a tall young officer in the uniform of the signal corps, his right arm in a heavy cast carried in a sling. The handsome face was marked with a deep scar across the left cheek. His smile was so pleading and boyish that I had to smile in spite of myself.

"All right," I said, holding my head high. "Just come along."

He introduced himself and chattered gaily, ignoring my cold replies, asking about the history of the castle and other famous spots. That did it. Anyone so interested in my beloved Golden City was my friend. I thawed out fast and soon we gossiped like old friends. I learned that Kurt was stationed in a military hospital near my school, had spent three terms of service at the Russian front, and expected to be sent out again.

"This time I don't have to travel far." His smile turned grim. "The Russian front is only a day's travel from here!"

He took me back to school that evening and asked gallantly to see me again. I had no desire to be around any men, but did not have the heart to turn him down. There was something about him that fascinated me though I couldn't figure it out. It took me several days to realize what was so unusual—the expression of his grey eyes.

He had the most contagious smile a person could have, but his eyes never smiled with his mouth. They were serious, intent, full of introverted emotions. As we learned to know each other better, I understood some of the reasons.

The memories of two Russian winters, being captured in Stalingrad, the wipe-out of his battalion where all of his comrades died and only he escaped, paying for that escape with two frozen feet and frozen parts of his face—it was obvious he had volunteered for war as a young, innocent boy; he had returned a sober, mature man.

One afternoon as we walked along Mala Strana, a famous street leading to the river where the towers of the Charles Bridge reached into the golden sky, he stopped and looked into my eyes.

"Hansi, I have never talked about this to anyone, but I want to share it with you. You remember when Stalingrad fell?"

I nodded. I could see it before me—we had hovered over the radio when the Fuhrer himself had announced the great tragedy and assured us that the death of our soldiers was the sure seed for our future victory.

"Well, my best friend was caught there." Kurt had a faraway stare. "We do not know yet if he died or was captured. But we have whispered tales among us that when the Russians closed the ring and we couldn't get through with food or mail any more except by air, that the last wireless messages we got from within was the call, "Send us Bibles! Send us Bibles!" Hansi, why on earth did our boys call for Bibles to help them die? I don't know much what a Bible is like; isn't it a Jewish book of some sort?"

I was too shocked to say much. "Kurt, did they give them Bibles?"

"Yes, they dropped all the Bibles that could be found. There were not many around, you know. One fellow who escaped after capture told me that our soldiers would beg for just one page to hold in their hands, and they would cry and read it and kiss it. Those poor fellows must have gone nuts to act like old women. I can't picture my friend like that at all. He was tall, proud, and strong and very idealistic. Just to think about it insults my memory of him."

We were crossing the Charles Bridge as we talked, and we stopped to look down into the deep green waters. I saw myself again standing behind the window the night the bomb had threatened that youth hospital. I remembered again the deep helplessness that had enveloped me in the face of death.

"Self-sacrifice is the highest fulfilment for a human being," I repeated slowly to Kurt. "That's what the Fuhrer taught us, didn't he?"

We stopped walking and I formed my thoughts into words with hesitance.

"I know the Bible, Kurt. I was brought up in a very religious foster home. It's a good book, but it is outdated and not relevant any more in our days. It is a book for cowards and weaklings."

My mind pictured Mother bent over the Bible by the flickering, dim light of an old lamp, and a sharp pain of guilt pierced through me. I felt that my words betrayed Mother, for she was no coward nor a weakling. I knew her inner strength, her noble thinking. But she and I had parted ways; I had left her and her beliefs and had given my undivided allegiance to the Fuhrer.

"Kurt, you faced death so often, what did *you* think when you thought of the end?"

Kurt's face resembled the carved stone faces above us. "I never faced it, little girl. I always knew that I would make it somehow, and I did! I don't care if it is highest fulfilment to die for the *Vaterland*; I don't want to. I want to live and enjoy life to the fullest, every moment of it. Life is shorter than a breeze and I want to squeeze out every pleasure possible. Life is cheating us, anyway!"

Suddenly I knew what Kurt carried in the depths of his eyes, something he had tried hard to hide: life-greediness. They all had it in their eyes, all those soldiers returning from Russia—Walter did, too—and Rudy! I began walking again.

"Kurt, do you know why I love this bridge so much?"

Kurt looked surprised. "What does this old bridge have to do with what we were talking about?"

My eyes followed the grey, carved stones of that most famous bridge, over 1600 feet long, dating back nearly six hundred years, and my hand caressed its aged smoothness. Gothic saint figures with flowing stone robes and golden haloes looked down on us in unhurried stoicism. Above us fortress Hradčany with its buttressed walls a thousand years old, and the cathedral in the glory of Gothic and baroque wealth soared into the sky. For me they were triumphant melodies in stone, timeless inspirations to mankind, a never-ending source of peace and security to my troubled heart as long as I had been in Prague.

"Kurt, we are standing in the midst of the past and the future. Look around. History comes alive. I love history, and history is the key to understanding life and death that we talked about. Man takes himself much too seriously. We are each just a small link in a chain, a string in the human web of long generations, and we live on forever in future generations. That *is* the answer to death, isn't it? Listen, Kurt, can't you hear how those old stones talk? They tell us that countless generations have walked this bridge before us. Mozart stood here and was inspired by this beauty to give us his great music. He is dead, but his music lives. The builders of the cathedral died long, long ago, but their work lives forever.

It's what we do that can live on after we die which gives meaning to life and death. And Stalingrad is a monument too—for future generations of our great Reich."

Kurt searched my face and I felt his eyes groping, but I avoided his hungry look and turned away from him. "Let's go back to school." I shivered. "It's getting cool!"

Silence stood between us on the way back. I knew what Kurt thought. He didn't care about the future or history. All he wanted was to live the present at its fullest. But I didn't feel that I could help him with that, and I deliberately closed all the doors to my heart.

There was no sense in giving anyone encouragement. I was not interested in anybody, not even my dear pen pals of many years—not even Walter. I had resumed correspondence with Walter and my Hitler Youth comrades who were not either missing or dead after four years of war, but I had nothing to give any of them but friendship, and I never made a secret of it. But I could not understand why I was not left alone by them. Kurt came back for more strolls and dates, and I enjoyed exploring the city with him. But why? My mail was voluminous and I could never write often enough to satisfy my correspondents. I finally discussed it with Walter in a letter. I found out that Walter had been engaged, too, and had broken the engagement after a short time as I had.

"Little Hansi," he wrote in reply to my question of why men asked for my friendship when I had so little to give, "you don't know what makes us males click, do you? You see, there are two types of girls in this world, the first type we seek out when we come back from war, eager to find pleasure and relief. The other type is the woman of our dreams, the girl we someday hope to marry. You are the girl men want to marry. For marriage is more than sex and flirtation; marriage is a friendship. I consider you my very best, maybe my *only* friend I have in this world. My engagement broke because I chose against better judgment. She had nothing to offer but bedroom furniture and herself in it. Out here in the misery of war we men don't want bedroom letters; we need more. We need what you offer. You care, and I know it. If I ever were in deepest trouble, I would come to you first, and you would never let me down. Friendship is the highest form of love, and your greatest gift to me is that you are true to your ideals. Don't ever change! No man will let you go because of this, Hansi. And I am the last one to give you up. Some day I shall come back."

I laid down my head and cried—cried for the first time since I had written my last letter to Rudy. Walter was wrong! Some men did let girls go who stay true to high ideals and believe in a great love! Some men use girls like trophies to build their masculine egos. Some men write beautiful letters, put a golden band on a girl's finger, but are not willing to accept the responsibility that comes with love. I sobbed out my bitterness and my loneliness and my frustration that I couldn't forget Rudy—because I still loved him and it was all so senseless and hard. But after that I felt better and my stomach didn't hurt quite so much all the time. I gained back some weight and was able to shoulder greater tasks. And just in time, for an unusual task needed my full strength.

# 6
## Twilight of the Gods

One day I had to report to a refugee children's home in the city. Berlin headquarters had given orders to evacuate all the children under government care from the city of Prague. I wondered why—but I had learned to follow orders without asking questions. I knew that the leaders of our Reich could be trusted.

I found about thirty children ready for the trip, with little knapsacks on their backs. In good spirits and eager to go for a train ride, they ranged in age from five to twelve years.

My written orders gave me the destination, time of train departures, and authority to use any train for transporting the entire group and myself.

Not until the youngsters formed marching ranks to leave did it dawn on me that I was solely responsible! No other adult could be freed to help me. I had thirty fidgety children and an order—that was it!

How I managed to get all those wiggly youngsters on the train I will never know, but somehow they got crammed in. When the conductor checked my papers he told me that we had to change trains in the next city. Oh dear, I didn't know that our final goal was way out in the country! A small cannon-ball train would take us there.

The bigger youngsters helped the little tots when it came to change trains. I got them all safely out, across some tracks and to the place where the country train puffed and hissed in full steam ready to leave. Then my heart sank. The train was stuffed full of people—Czech people mostly—who eyed my large group and me with open hostility. I explained the situation to the conductor, but he pretended not to hear. I went to the station manager and showed my papers. He didn't even look, but slowly raised his disk to give the signal for the train to leave. Some of the children began to cry and I got very scared and very angry.

"Sir," I said in the Czech language, "if you let this train go without putting these children on, I shall call for SS help!"

The change in that man flabbergasted me. The train had started to move, but he blew a shrill whistle and the train halted. The official screamed some orders into one railway car and the passengers grabbed their luggage and stepped out, wordlessly, making room for the children to board the train. I said a friendly thank you in Czech but there was no reply—just faces of stone. The station manager raised the disk again and the train pulled out.

After roll call to account for all the children, I opened the window to look back, and saw some displaced passengers shake their fists at me.

I squeezed myself in beside the smallest child in my group and the little curly-haired tot put her head trustingly in my lap. She was tired. So was I—tired and bewildered. I felt terribly guilty and didn't know why. Or did I? For the first time in my life I had used my authority as a Nazi leader to threaten someone and the reaction to my threat was harder to take than the fear of being stranded with thirty children—the fear which had motivated me to yell at the man in the first place.

My thoughts tumbled. Why had the Czech people obeyed without protest? Were they *that* afraid of the SS troops? Of course, the SS was the arm of Hitler's authority in all the land, but they were only obeying orders, just as I did. I was responsible for those helpless children, wasn't I? But my feeling of guilt grew and I felt as if I had betrayed someone, but I didn't know who it was.

When we finally arrived at the small city where a new, makeshift children's home waited for those refugees from the east, the air raid sirens were screaming alarm. The children crowded around me at the depot while the train pulled away in haste. The railway station was completely deserted so I led the group to the air-raid shelter nearby, but the door was locked from the inside. The children wailed. I got their attention and ordered total silence, then I explained our next moves. The children would line up in single file, hold hands, and follow me. No noise, just walking fast in the shadow of the apartment houses, close to the walls so we couldn't be so easily seen. If the planes attacked we had to lie flat behind any shelter available or just lie flat on the sidewalk.

The many little feet moved in rhythm behind me as I led. There was no other noise or sign of life on the street except all those small wooden soles tapping sharply in the dead silence— *eins-zwei, eins-zwei*—and in the distance the mean rumble of planes—bombers. They sounded like Father's bees. As they came nearer, nearer, nearer, my childhood panic grabbed me. I wanted to run, run, run! But I remembered Mother's words; "*Marichen*, don't run, bees sting only when you fight or run. Stand still, stand still, and the bees will go away!'

I stopped, and thirty pairs of feet stopped dead with me. I motioned for the children to step back deeper into the shadow of the buildings. As the airplanes droned nearer I thought I could not only smell the chemical stench of exploding bombs, but also smoke and torn human flesh. Then the planes' hum got softer, friendlier, and was gone without attack. The sirens screamed a high-pitched signal that the danger had passed for the moment.

One hour later the children sat around tables and eagerly sipped hot soup. It was meagre fare for dinner, but they knew nothing better and they were happy and relieved. So was I. I could return and report: *"Befehl ausgeführt* (order fulfilled). I had done what was expected of me——but why did I feel so horribly guilty about threatening that Czech railway official? After all, what choice did I have? Was there any choice in the world?

One day at the end of March 1945 we got orders from headquarters to leave Prague immediately and go home. Perplexed, I reported to my leader in charge and asked for permission to stay. First of all, I had no place to go, and besides, there was still so much work to do. How could we all leave?

My *Fuhrerin* shook her head firmly. "No, Maria Anne; orders are orders. The city is no longer safe for you girls. The Russians are standing east of Prague."

I shook my head naively. "Why worry about that? Hitler will never let Prague be conquered by the enemy. He loves this city!" Had he not spoken over the radio the day before and promised that victory would come soon? With the new miracle weapons our German scientists were getting ready, Germany would be able to rout our enemies within days. The end of the was was in sight. Couldn't I stay?

"My girl, you must leave today," she replied. "Don't you have any relatives?"

"Yes, my sister in Reichenberg. I don't know her very well because we did not meet each other until a couple of years ago. Her husband fell on the battlefield in Russia. Maybe I could stay with her for a few weeks until I come back to school."

The railway station had no answering service, so I had to go on the streetcar to find out about the possibility of trains leaving. I also stopped by the military hospital and told Kurt good-bye.

The trains no longer ran on schedule; everything was chaos. But I was told there might be a train leaving that night, so I went back to the school to get my things.

My superior wrote an emergency ticket for the train and I left, wondering about the strange expression on her face as I bade her *"Auf Wiedersehen."*

My suitcase in one hand and the last day's mail in the other, I made my way to the railway station. The air seemed tense with hositility and foreboding. Perched in the overcrowded streetcar, I ignored the hostile glances I got from the Czechs. I was too occupied with my own worries.

I had a card from Walter, scribbled partially by him but finished by a nurse. He had been badly wounded again and was in an emergency hospital at a harbour city of Lithuania. There the wounded waited for troop transport ships to take them to northern Germany. His words contrasted starkly with his weak handwriting—a message of joy that he was coming home.

Then all at once it hit me—the news I hadn't paid attention to the day before. The Russians had torpedoed several hospital ships a few days ago. The ships had been clearly marked as hospital ships and were loaded with hundreds of wounded soldiers and officers from Lithuania to northern Germany. There were no survivors.

No, it couldn't be! Walter hadn't gone through all that hell of war for five long years to be murdered when he was helpless, wounded, and jubilantly on his way home? He was the only son, the idol of his proud, well-to-do parents. I couldn't picture that handsome face of his fighting with the icy waters of the Baltic Sea, going down, down into a watery grave. No, no, no! It was too cruel to be true. Tears overwhelmed me; I couldn't hold them back. Times had passed when I was too proud and strong to cry. Five years of war had left my soul bruised and raw; I was numb and confused from all the heartaches, and tears were welcome relief.

The trip was long and often interrupted. Fighter planes attacked our moving train and left the railcars stranded on the tracks for most of the night. Passengers cried, cursed, moaned, and prayed while I sat motionless at the window staring into the dark.

Reality was slipping away and I felt like an actress on a stage, pushed into a play by an unseen power. But I didn't know my lines; I was like a puppet manipulated by an outside force. I knew nothing of what the next act would bring. I felt helpless.

In my mind I could even hear the music to the play—Richard Wagner's. His was my favourite music, though I often wondered if I had favoured him first because he was Adolf Hitler's most loved composer. Wagner's music had become part of my life and my emotions. Yes, I could hear it, the motif of the "Trauermarsch" from *Gotterdämmerung* (Twilight of the Gods). My spirit longed to be brave, but premonition and loneliness nearly suffocated me.

Why couldn't I be without fear of death like my favourite heroine in the Nibelungen epic? Brunnhilde, Wagner's Valkyrie. I could never hear Wagner's dramatic opera music about her without shivering in awe. Why did Hitler love *Der Nibelungenring* the most? The end of it was dissolution, nothingness, death by choice. Why would he teach us by his example to love music of annihilation when he was building a Reich for a thousand years? Why was life filled with conflict and contradiction? How long would I have to wait before I could go back to Prague?

O Prague, you great prima donna! I am eager to go back and live in the shadow of your beauty, listen to your heartbeat and discover more of your ancient, wise soul. Why, oh, why did I have to leave that place that seemed more like home to me than any spot in the world?

Margret looked weary and the children skinny and listless when I walked into their little house. Food was terribly scarce and I was suddenly one more mouth to feed—no wonder I didn't get a joyful reception. I determined to leave as soon as possible, but where could I go? Gloom and foreboding filled the air, while a clock ticked the time slowly away and the flower-painted cupboards in Margret's tiny kitchen showed more and more empty spaces. We all seemed to be waiting, numbly waiting—for what?

# 7
## *Crushed*

Weeks later I learned the Russians had entered the eastern edge of Prague a few hours after I left. My train must have been one of the last to pull out of the terminal unhindered before the terrible blood bath took place that reports described as inhuman.

Czech nationalists killed hundreds of Nazis and fought the German troops savagely while the Russians held back at the east side of Prague to let their Czech friends do the dirty work. Death had missed me again. Why? Most likely the woman who had forced me to leave and had saved my life lost hers, for she stayed.

Only one day after my arrival at my sister's, Kurt stood before me again. I thought I was seeing a ghost!

"What are you doing here, young man?" I demanded.

"I came with the same train you did." Kurt had his impish grin again. "I just couldn't get to you because the train was so overcrowded. They shipped me to a safer place to get well so I can fight again.' He grimaced and laughed.

I had a feeling that Kurt had pulled some strings or just walked out of that hospital in Prague after I had told him good-bye. Whatever the case, he was alive because of it, and I was grateful for that.

Kurt and I saw much of each other for several weeks. He was so pleased when time came for his cast to be removed. He exercised his fingers by the hour and he could use both hands again.

One balmy evening we walked through the park and sat down under a blooming jasmine bush. The air was heavy with its intoxicating fragrance. Kurt looked at me and said bluntly, "Let's get married, Hansi—tomorrow!"

I laughed in his face.

"I'm not joking, girl," he said, irritated. I mean it. We can get our licence within twenty-four hours. You know how fast the military works by now. We can be married by tomorrow night!"

"That might be so, Kurt," I smiled, "but why should we get married?"

"Because I want to sleep with you!"

"But, Kurt, that is no ground for marriage." I felt myself blushing. "You should know me by now. I marry only because of love, and we are not in love!"

"Maybe not. I know you are not; maybe I love you. All I know is that I want you and I can't have you unless I marry you!"

I laughed again. "Kurt, you couldn't get me whether married or unmarried unless I was ready for you. Why would you go through all the trouble of marrying me just to have me? There are enough girls in this city who will be yours for the asking!"

"That may be so, Maria Anne, but I don't want any of them. I want you. And I want you more than anything I ever wanted in my life; I can't eat or sleep any more, you are so much on my mind!"

I could understand how Kurt felt, for there had once been a

6

man in my life who possessed my heart that much. But such love was not real. It ended in disillusionment and pain.

I shook my head. "No, Kurt, I would never do that to you; I doubt that I ever marry."

"Is it because you still love that Navy man?"

"No, I don't think so, Kurt." I felt very defensive. "Actually, he wasn't even my type. I don't go for brown hair and dark eyes; I go for the German type!"

"Well, at least I qualify by eye·and hair colour," Kurt said sarcastically, but I interrupted him.

"Kurt, have I ever quoted you my favourite saying?"

"Oh, you quoted so many sayings to me, little dreamer, but I don't know which one of your favourites·you mean."

*"Rein bleiben und reif werden, das ist höchste·und edelste Lebenskunst."* (To stay pure and become mature, that is the highest and most noble art of life.)

"You are a hopeless dreamer, girl," Kurt said, very agitated. "Look, dear, the Russians are already close to this city. I have to leave the day after tomorrow. If you listen closely you can already hear the rumble of the artillery. Wake up, girl, life is just about over for you and me!"

"What do you mean?" I cried. "Life is over? Sure, it will take some more hard weeks to finish this war, but we'll be fine after that. As soon as our new miracle weapons are brought in, the Russians will leave and I can go back to school!"

Kurt gave me an incredulous look. "Hansi," he said very kindly, "the Russians will be in this city, right here, within days or short weeks. Nothing will stop them. Stop waiting for Hitler. Why don't you live it up with me—we have so little time left— all you've known in your young life is hardship and duties. Hansi, today we live, who knows when we die!"

"No, Kurt," I said and big tears burned my cheeks. "You are wrong! I shall not doubt my country and Hitler nor our victory. You don't know what you are saying. Those many friends of mine who died for our cause—how can it all end in death and defeat? Never, Kurt, never! As for you and me, I am your friend for life. That's all I have to give!"

Kurt jumped to his feet and for the first time I watched him lose control of a temper I didn't know he had.

"Fine, you dumb girl," he shouted. "Go ahead and save your ideals for the Russians! Your pure body, your dreams, all of it! They will rape you and teach you! Just wait for them. Save yourself for the Russian hordes. Just save it all for them!"

He stomped away and left me behind with his words ringing in my ears but not making sense. Kurt had gone mad to even think such horrid things and I sat and tried to understand why he would threaten me so. But it was hard to reason it out.

He came back the next day and apologized and I saw him off the following morning as he left for war again. There was no smile on his face, only resentment. His eyes shouted the same words in silence that he had screamed at me under the tree, but he said nothing, and I knew that he was wrong.

On another beautiful day shortly after Kurt left, Admiral Doenitz, Rudy's commander, spoke over the air. We sat before my sister's radio and listened intently. Doenitz had, by Hitler's last will, taken the reins of our leaderless nation to carry on. In a matter of hours, even though it was not officially announced, the whole country knew and whispered from door to door that Hitler and his mistress Eva Braun had committed suicide!

We were stunned. Why would Hitler do such a ghastly thing? Hadn't he promised to lead us to victory? Still, I didn't question Hitler's decision. I couldn't understand, but I trusted that our hero knew what was best for the nation and in that mysterious act of "self-sacrifice" had shown a way for us. I could not entertain the thought that Hitler, my god and idol, could have used a coward's way out of a predicament of his own making.

Two days later the Russians marched into Reichenberg. I

stared into those strange faces as the soldiers tramped and rode in past my sister's house toward the city centre. I stood behind the window curtains and watched, numb with fright and unbelief, and waited! Yes, I knew that Hitler was dead—but I still trusted him. I knew that Hitler's promises would be fulfilled; it was only a matter of time!

When Admiral Doenitz announced the total surrender of Germany to the Allies, my stupefied mind refused to believe it. I picked up the screaming baby and held her while the radio blared its mad message. Mechanically I did what was expected of me, but I could neither speak nor bring order into my thinking. I felt myself falling into a bottomless pit and I knew I was dreaming a horrible nightmare. Soon I would wake up, wouldn't I?

The nightmare seemed to get worse. The children begged for food, but we had only enough to feed them once a day. In the nights we could hear women scream in neighbouring houses, and we knew that Russians were on raping forays. My sister and I didn't dare sleep at the same time; we would take turns staying awake to listen. As soon as we heard steps approach our house we would hide. And as I hovered in dark corners of my sister's attic, shaking with fear, hiding myself every night, I would hear Kurt's shout: "Go ahead, save yourself for the Russian hordes. Save yourself for them!"

It was only a question of time before I would be hunted down by the lustful, drunken soldiers. I would rather die than let myself be touched by one of those brutes. No, Kurt, I might have been a foolish dreamer, but nobody would ever degrade me that much. I wouldn't let them. Maybe I should follow my friends and Hitler to the last and die by choice. But was it right to kill myself? For what cause would I die? Was there anything left in this world to live for? Save yourself—die—for what?

I was not the only one who felt past all hope and full of

despair. Many Germans did what I contemplated; they followed Hitler to the bitter end and committed suicide.

One of my former summer chiefs in the department of NSV (Nazi welfare work) had been a friend to me up to the day of the Russian occupation. I had gone to him after Kurt had threatened me about the future, and Mr. Braun had reassured me that victory of Germany was sure. It couldn't be any other way. I knew that he meant it. He believed in the Fuhrer with as much fervour and dedication as I did—or more. When the total surrender of the German Third Reich ended its existence, he and his devoted wife prepared a last good meal for themselves and their five children. They put poison into the last dish and never got up from the table. They were found after days, slumped over their empty plates, horribly discoloured from the poison. Other Nazis didn't have to take their own lives; someone else did the job for them.

One day after the surrender, I was compelled with many other women to work for the local Communist administration. We were assigned the task of weeding around the city crematorium, a busy place during those days. There were so many corpses to dispose of, and the chimney billowed smoke.

All at once our monotonous work was interrupted by some terrible screams from the inside of the building. We were all used to screams by then. Women screamed at night when soldiers broke into the German home for rape and robbing. People screamed when the Russians decided to raid streets or public places for Germans who had forgotten their white arm bands which marked all of us as *Nemci* (Germans) and made us defenceless "game" for anyone who felt like hunting. Screams we were accustomed to by then, but those moaning cries sent chills down my spine. Such agonized wails by a deep masculine voice—what could have happened?

After a while two Czech National Guards brought a man out from the crematorium. We recognized him as Dr. Helmer, a well-known German physician of the city and a prominent figure of the Nazi regime. As he was led away, he wept and groaned loudly, wringing his handcuffed hands in hopeless agony.

Later a Czech city employee told us that during the night someone had forced himself into the Helmer home and strangled the mother and four children. Then to make sure that all were dead, the killer had cut their throats. All five bodies had been brought to the crematorium, and then the authorities had brought Dr. Helmer from imprisonment in a Communist labour camp to identify the victims.

"They didn't warn that poor man beforehand either," said the Czech employee indignantly. He seemed deeply moved by the heartbroken expression of grief we all had seen and heard. "It is not right to treat anyone like that. And what is it the four little children did that they had to die so horribly?"

We nodded, but nobody answered. We Germans knew better than to say anything, for we could have been shot if we had expressed the same thoughts. But what a storm I hid behind my impassive face!

How was it possible that life could have become such a cruel nightmare from one week to the next? How much could a person stand before cracking up? For several days and nights those screams stayed with me, tortured me, frustrated me with the great "why" about the meaning of suffering and death. There was no answer as I stared in the darkness of the tiny attic I squeezed into while hiding at nights to escape prowling soldiers.

I felt myself falling into a deep abyss of confusion, and my derangement became so intense that I felt as if I were two persons. One was numb with fear and shuddered about all I had to witness; the second watched the first in amazed unbelief, sure that I was only dreaming and would wake up soon to my orderly, idealistic life of the immediate past. But the nightmare held on, and I felt myself falling deeper into horror and bottom-less darkness. I thought my cup of woe was full and I would have to end my life if more would be added, but I did not know about the tenacity and the instinct of self-preservation in a young life.

# 8
## Slave Women

One morning I was required to report at a Communist labour
centre for the usual daily assignment in the city. But soon I
found myself perched high on an open truck with many other
girls and women. We were swiftly transported across the
German-Czech line deep into the interior of Old Bohemia. By
late afternoon we arrived at a huge farm, Communist style. The
place had several buildings, including large barns. Surround-
ing the farm was a high stone wall with two gates. Evidently the
estate had been the manorial domain of a rich Czech proprietor,
recently confiscated.

The new manager and overseers, we soon discovered, had
been picked from the ranks of the farmhands who had served
the land owner. These new bosses had little aptitude for their
positions but attempted to compensate with shouting and arbit-
rary orders.

Dazed from hunger, we climbed off the vehicle and faced a
brute of a man, our new overseer. He shouted some commands,
and I understood that we were supposed to climb up a shaky
ladder that led into a kind of attic in the barn. There we found
a few old cots, and some fresh straw spread on the floor—our
new sleeping quarters!

In my heart raged a storm of hate. Realizing how easily they had tricked me into a labour camp, I hated myself for having been so gullible. I looked around. There was no chance of escape; we were far from German territory. The white band on the left sleeve marked us as Germans. The walls were high, and the whole place swarmed with hostile, suspicious people. We had no choice; we might as well submit quietly.

The next morning, after a meagre breakfast, we were ordered at sunrise into the fields. The new regime demanded production, and our overseer was more than eager to put on a good show. He rushed us mercilessly from the first minute.

We worked doggedly. My suppressed fury speeded my work. As the sun rose, the heat became unbearable; we had no water. Putting my rake down, I crossed the field and faced the sullen overseer. "The girls need water or they will not be able to work very well," I said in Czech. "We are dizzy, and some will faint." His eyes and mine met for some seconds.

I thought he was getting ready to strike me, but instead he forced a sly smile on his face and replied, "Very well, you girls shall have some water, just because you asked for it, Manjo (Czech for Mary). I see that you are a fast worker, Manjo. I hope you will become my helper in many ways!"

I turned silently and walked back to my work, thinking, "Who does he think I am? His 'helper,' ha!"

"Control yourself, girl; control yourself," I murmured as I dug my nails into my clenched fists. I had to learn to be quiet or it would make things worse for me and the others.

We got drinking water that first day; but there were other days when the man's ugly mood controlled him, and we had to work without water. Girls fainted, women screamed, and the frustrated overseer used his fists to urge us on. But he never bothered me. Somehow he treated me with reluctant respect and left me alone. He knew that the girls had made me their spokesman, and my influence on them could be felt as we reached our work quota. I had the girls organized so that two or more able workers would take a weak or unskilled girl in the middle. As soon as a girl lagged behind, we faster workers stepped in and helped her so she could catch up. This way we protected each other from beatings most of the time.

In spite of our efforts, our group diminished in size. Nobody bothered to discuss it. Life had become a nightmare of hunger, thirst, hard work, and fear.

The days would have been bearable, but the nights! A few days after we arrived, the soldiers stationed in the next village found out about our German girl group. That night they broke into our sleeping quarters, led by our grinning overseer. I was one of the few who got away unmolested.

The following night the Russians were back in larger numbers. It was impossible for any of us to hide or to get away; they had stationed a soldier with a cocked gun below the ladder.

I felt my blood drain from my face, and my knees shook. Again I had that incredible feeling that it was not really me facing those drunken, vulgar intruders, but that I watched in unbelief a horror play enacted on the stage of life. I knew not the outcome of the drama, but only one thing. I would not let them touch me; I would rather die.

By the dim moonlight filtering through a high window, and by the light of their flashlights, the soldiers mustered us girls. My best friends among the girls cried, "Manjo! Talk to them! Tell them we are Czechoslovakian girls, not Germans."

Yes, it was true we were Czechoslovakian citizens, but because our mother tongue was German, the Czechs didn't claim us anymore. The hate of those days exceeded belief.

I didn't speak Russian, but Czech is related enough to the Russian language that I could communicate on a limited scale. I faced the soldiers and shrieked, "Leave us alone! We are Czechoslovakians!"

Most of the Russians drew back. Into their brains, befuddled with drink and passion, struck the word "Czech." They knew better than to assault Czech girls. They could be court-martialled for that and they knew it—so did we!

One soldier called the overseer.

"Tell them that we are Czechoslovakians," I pleaded with that leering man. "Please, tell them. They will go away if you say it, and it is true!"

The overseer gave me a malicious sneer, then he turned to the soldiers. "They are *Nemci*," he said. "Have them!"

Hate towards that spiteful man surged so intensely I forgot my fear. "You beast," I hissed, and bit my lips so hard I could taste blood. "You ugly beast!"

The overseer turned abruptly away and left us with the Russians. The soldiers grabbed again. As one pulled by friend Helga from my side, she held on to me.

"Please, leave her alone," I begged. "Please don't harm her!" I spoke Czech.

The Russian had already thrown her on a cot and pinned her down with one elbow while holding on to a pistol with the other hand. She still clung to my hand, pulling me towards both of them.

"If you don't keep your mouth shut, you'll be next," the soldier told me with a contemptuous, appraising look. He talked in Russian, but I could understand all too well. His expression told me what words failed to communicate. He turned his attention back toward Helga.

His foul breath struck my face. Nausea choked me breathless but I held on to Helga's hand. "Helga, don't fight. He will kill you," I begged her over and over.

Helga didn't fight. She lay still, her face like a white stone. I watched that Russian defile my friend and my thoughts tumbled like a rockslide down the mountains.

Was *this* what my teachers had called highest fulfilment of womanhood? Had I kept myself untouched through all my teen life to end up like this? If this was part of the human life, I would never want any of it. It was revolting, animalistic, violent. Another ideal was transmuted into a dirty lie. Sex was not at the end of a rainbow dream as I had thought. Sex was raw lust acted out before my eyes by a drunken soldier who dared to use my best friend for it, and I shook with hate and disgust.

When the soldiers finally left, we girls huddled together like frightened little animals and whispered with each other. "Manjo, you're the lucky one—the Russians don't want you because you are·so skinny," one girl said who had been raped by four soldiers that night. She was endowed with voluptuous curves, and I had often envied her for it.

Another girl who had not been raped followed the thought. "It's true, they picked only the curvy girls tonight. Maybe it's not so bad after all to be flat and skinny?"

It sounded incredible. That couldn't be the only reason why she and I had got away untouched. There had to be something more to it than that—but what? I thought of the many stories I had heard before I came to this place.

My sister's mother-in-law, a woman in her late sixties, had been molested and hurt so badly that she bled for days. My great-uncle, a man I had never met, had to watch drunken Russians assault his wife and his twelve-year-old granddaughter.

I looked at Helga. She·didn't speak at all. I knew her life story; she had been engaged to an officer of the German air force and had twice missed her wedding by days. The second time was just before the Russians broke into the city. All she ever thought or talked about was her handsome fiancé and her future with him.

"Helga, don't take it so hard," I whispered. But I didn't sound convincing, only surprised that the girls who had been raped were willing to go on living and able to talk about it.

"Manjo, what if I get pregnant?" Helga whispered, and she

sounded so desperate. "And what will my Werner say?"

"Don't think about it," I answered. "Someday life has to be better again and you . . ." My voice trailed off—what could I say?

As the weeks went by, I suffered with Helga as I watched her fight the morning sickness of a dreaded pregnancy. . . .

Life after that night became more and more of a nightmare. Our chances for undisturbed sleep were slim. Shame and death seemed close from one moment to the next. Nothing kept me going but pride, hatred, and stubbornness. I was more determined than ever that I would never surrender to anyone, but would fight and scratch like a wildcat until they shot me.

So far, I had never needed to fight to protect myself. Did some unseen power take care of me? It seemed so. The other girls noticed and asked, "Manjo, what kind of good luck charm do you have? Nothing happens to you. The overseer is leaving you alone, and the soldiers don't bother you. You never faint in the fields."

"Nonsense," I replied. "You know better than to be superstitious. Good luck charms are old women's tales. There is nothing special about me."

But deep inside, I began to wonder. It was the same feeling Rudy had told me about once when he survived so many close calls. Something really seemed to protect me, but what? The religious convictions of my childhood had been so thoroughly brainwashed out of me that it did not occur to me that God might have been my Defender. The whole situation seemed so incomprehensible, but it was real.

On the other hand, I didn't know how long my good fortune would last, and I was not eager to take any chances. After that first visit of the soldiers I began to look around with a purpose. We knew they would be back again, and we knew that nobody would bother to stop them. The overseer seemed pleased that he could be of service to his Russian friends. The other girls and women depended on me for advice and help. It was almost as if they had made me their lucky charm. So I had to find a solution.

The first thing to do was to find a hiding place. But where? We had to stay within the court because the gates were locked at night, and the Russians enforced a merciless curfew. Czechs, Slovenians, and Germans alike were subject to it.

Then I found it. At the far end of the large farmyard stood an old barn half filled with straw and hay. The building could be entered by a small side door after the large doors were closed at night. We tried it. Late every evening when we could hear the overseer snoring, we noiselessly climbed down our old chicken ladder, sneaked across the courtyard one by one, and slipped cautiously through the small door into the straw. We dug individual "caves" in the fresh straw, and it seemed more comfortable than in our former sleeping quarters. Each night the entire group migrated to this place, where we enjoyed better rest and greater security.

With the coming of summer heat, tensions mounted and tempers grew short. We thought of little else than our need for more food and rest. We stopped counting days. We had no calendar. We staggered through the days with scarcely a thought for the morrow, because all was hopeless.

One day in midsummer everything went wrong. We were not permitted to take water out, and the heat had become sultry and oppressive. Thunderclouds threatened the ripening grain and made the overseer nervous. Before our eyes he hit a young mother, who had stopped raking to still her fussing child. I could hardly bear to watch it without retaliation. We listened to the cries of mother and child. Then we quarrelled among ourselves, and some girls cried.

Sunburned and exhausted, we finally dragged ourselves back to our quarters where, after a few bites of poor food, we climbed the ladder to the straw. Desperately I fought off sleep after we retired, because I knew that I must awaken the girls for our excursion to the barn. It was especially important that night, for new Russian troops had been coming in that afternoon, and some soldiers had seen us as we worked in a field beside the country road. Some soldiers had even stopped to inquire of the overseer. Those soldiers would know before evening where we could be found. I couldn't afford to go to sleep; I had to get us all out in time.

As I dozed off, my mind began to wander. I could hardly believe that it had been just a year since I had taken part in that summer aid programme in the Sudeten mountains. Yes, and it would soon be a year from the time when Rudy had come to that remote spot and we had run across the flowery pasture under smiling sunshine and fluffy white clouds. I could hear myself saying to him, "Rudy, tell me that I am not just dreaming. Oh, Rudy!"

How hard I had tried not to think of him during the past few months. What had become of him? Was he still alive? Maybe his U-boat had been blown up as so many had shortly before the end of the war. If his boat had come back, where was he? Maybe in a prison camp? How had he taken Germany's defeat? He had been such an optimistic and enthusiastic Nazi. Neither of us had even considered the possibility of a German defeat. Maybe he had committed suicide like some other officers. As I saw it, suicide might be the most noble way out of the whole mess, and I had considered it several times, especially since I had been pressed into this labour camp. But how could a person do it? I had no gun or fast-acting poison. Besides, *was* it really a noble way out? Mother would say that it would be an escape for cowards.

What about Mother? Most likely she was dead. I hadn't seen her for five years. Frail little woman, how much chance would she have had in these last months of starvation and suffering? Father was gone, for sure. He had depended upon medicine and doctor's care from day to day. It was comforting for me to picture those I loved as being dead. Better that than to go through days like mine.

Maybe Rudy had been caught by the Russians. No, I wanted him to be dead, too; not hungry as I was and hunted like a defenceless animal. It seemed so desirable to be dead!

Quietly I got up and awakened the girls. Accustomed by then to climb noiselessly down the wobbly ladder, we made our way quickly over to the barn. As I reached out both hands to open the squeaky side door, something warned me against going in. Was it a voice? Surprised, I turned around. Behind me stood the silent group of girls huddled together in fright.

I shook my head in disgust. "Manjo," I thought, "you are getting crazy and you are beginning to hear ghosts."

Again I stepped forward to enter and a second time something seemed to say within me, "Don't go into that barn tonight."

In an instant I had decided. My deep urge was clear and strong, and while I could not understand who or what was warning me, I knew I felt the same way as when I had left Mother and when I had said good-bye to Rudy. I knew that I had to obey that voice.

I whispered to the waiting girls, "I won't go in tonight."

"Why not, Manjo? We are so tired and want to go back to sleep. Look! We have been safe in that barn for many nights!" The girls began to whisper and get noisy.

"Hush," I said firmly. "You all may go in—I will not stop you. It's only that I don't want to go in myself, that's all."

The girls were undecided, but then one girl said, "Oh, no. If Manjo doesn't go into the barn tonight, I will not go either. She usually knows what she is doing."

Nobody wanted to enter that barn. But what to do next? The same inner urge seemed to tell me. "We must leave these premises tonight," I whispered, and began to walk quietly towards the locked east gate. The girls followed me. One of my closest friends among the group hurried close to my side and whispered in fright, "Hansi, have you forgotten curfew? I hope you know what you are doing! Do you realize what a chance we are taking? Nobody is allowed out after 9.30, not even the Czech people!"

Had I fogotten curfew? Will I ever forget to the day I die what curfew means? Shot without warning if anyone with a gun saw us outside the wall. Oh, I knew, I knew! I nodded impatiently.

"Yes, Lilo, I know. But somehow I just feel we must get out of here for tonight. I don't know how to explain it. Please don't ask me any more questions, for we must hurry."

I had learned how to open the gate some days before through a kind Czech woman who had secretly befriended me. Quickly I had the mechanism released, and through the slightly open gate the frightened girls slipped out into the fields. As soon as I had closed the gate, I followed the group. The night was still, and the moon and stars seemed cruel in their brightness, for they betrayed our moving forms. Close to the woods we found a field where we had harvested alfalfa a few days before. The hay had been stacked on high wooden racks to dry out. I suggested that the girls crawl under those haystacks for protection and a little sleep. The girls obeyed without delay. Lilo and I also squeezed under one of the stacks and tried to make ourselves comfortable. But sleep stayed away that night. Death seemed near enough to touch and we were tense and apprehensive. The frogs croaked loudly in a nearby pond. Other night noises from the woods sounded strange and forbidding. We heard the barking of dogs, now closer, now fading into the distance again, as we sat with cramped muscles and waited.

At last the stars began to pale into deep darkness, then we could see signs of day in the east. Dawn was our salvation,

Z

because we knew that every Russian soldier had to return by morning light, and their army discipline was very strict. They would have left by the time we crept back to our sleeping quarters at the labour camp.

We managed to get back in time without being detected by the overseer. After a short while he blew the whistle and we all "got up" and formed our routine line for report and breakfast.

I was very unhappy with myself. Why hadn't I let the girls sleep in the straw barn last night? Now we were all so dead tired from the crazy goose chase I started. Nothing could have happened in the night, for the night was gone and around me was a glorious sunrise, awakening birds, and a thousand dew diamonds sparkling in the morning glow. I was stupid—and I felt sure the girls thought so too. Was I going crazy?

With more disgust than usual I noticed the breakfast menu —soup, consisting mainly of water and salt and some potatoes, and some crusts of dry bread. I couldn't help wondering if the cook let the bread mould systematically before he portioned it out to us in stingy rations. How could any kitchen produce so much spoiled bread at all times without deliberate planning?

Well, it really didn't matter; we were hungry enough to devour anything edible. As the line began to move, I eagerly awaited my turn because my stomach hurt so much when I was hungry. Suddenly I felt a gentle nudge in my ribs. Looking up, I saw the kind face of that Czech woman who had been our secret friend.

"*Devcatko*" (little girl), she whispered, trying to appear inconspicuous, "I got to tell you something!"

"*Ano?*" (yes) I mumbled.

"The Russians were here last night!"

I nodded, unimpressed. Her words were really no news at all.

"Listen, Manjo. It was really very bad!" She pointed toward the kitchen. "One of those women over there betrayed you last night. She told those drunken soldiers where you have been hiding. Oh, those sons of the devil." She crossed herself fearfully. "They were so mad because they couldn't find you and made so much commotion. Do you know what they did? Those *hloupy Rucky* (stupid Russian) beasts got into the barn where you have been sleeping and looked through the straw. When they were not able to find you, they used their bayonets to jab through the straw, swearing and shouting, 'Those German pigs will squeak when we stab them!'

"Though they hunted for you the whole night," she continued, "they couldn't find you anywhere. In the name of our holy saint, where did you hide? I shall burn a candle to our Holy Madonna next Sunday for protecting you. Oh, you poor *Nemci*, I am glad that you are not hurt.'

I was so horrified I felt dizzy. As she hurried off, I stammered a soft *"Dekuji"* (thank you) after her.

So it was known that we had been hiding in the barn! But who had told me not to go in last night?

I passed the news to the girls around me and their whispering went like the morning wind down the line on both sides of me. Carefully, slowly, in order not to arouse our overseer's suspicion, the girls crowded around me and implored, "Manjo, how did you know? Manjo, who told you that we shouldn't sleep in that barn last night? Manjo, what charm do you use?"

I shrugged. "I don't know, girls; I really don't know. It was just—well, I can't explain it!"

The line moved quickly on because the overseer yelled and whistled impatiently. Receiving my soup, I drank it hurriedly. I tried to bring order into my muddled brain while I chewed my hard crust of *chleb* (bread), but it was no use. Everything seemed hazy, and I couldn't channel my thinking in the right direction. Something had gone wrong with me. My memory did not work!

I tried to reach back into my thoughts, to tie past and present together, but it was no use. I tried to remember some basic things like home or Mother or the one I loved, and couldn't. Worst of all, those figures suddenly lacked names. No, it was not possible. I couldn't have forgotten Mother's name. Oh, what was Mother's name?

Obviously I was going crazy. Maybe soon my aching head would burst, and I would do something irrational and go hysterical. I knew what that would mean. If I cracked up like others I had known—the solution was simple: one or two bullets.

No, I had to get away from my persecutors while I could still make decisions. I wouldn't surrender and give that ugly overseer the devilish satisfaction that he had broken me—that he had won! No, I would fight, escape, leave, walk out. If they killed me, all right—at least it wasn't a surrender!

As soon as we arrived at our assigned place of work, I announced my departure to the girls around me. Some wanted to go with me, and I grimly nodded my agreement.

We looked at the direction of wind and sun; then when the overseer had left our field, we deliberately walked away. Woods are plentiful in Bohemia, and we hurried towards the nearest one. As soon as we had reached the dark coolness of the dense evergreens, we moved steadily northward, listening anxiously for any threatening noises.

Our overseer must have felt very sure of himself. He knew how deep we were in Czech territory. He knew also that Russian soldiers combed the area for escaped prisoners everywhere. He knew we would be caught sooner or later and be brought back.

I do not know how long we walked and hid and struggled through woods and fields. That whole escape is one grey haze of terror and endless walk in my memory. All I know is that we did reach the Sudeten territory, and the girls left one by one to seek their separate havens. At last I arrived at my sister's.

My sister Margret asked few questions after she had cautiously opened the door to answer my knocking. She quietly led me upstairs where I could hide and sleep undisturbed. I fell upon the mattress, and she removed my shoes. Her motherly hand put a blanket over me, and while I sank into deep sleep I mumbled into the pillow, "Everything is shattered, Sis; all broken up. But things will be all right after I wake up. It's just a bad dream I am having."

# 9
## Farewell

I woke up startled. Where was I? Sunbeams forced their way through the cracks of the attic and hushed voices came from far away. Oh, yes, I was at my sister's place hiding and I must have slept very late.

I tried to get up. My body ached. On blistered feet I hobbled out of the room and down the stairs.

The children raced to embrace me, and the baby girl, Uta, gurgled with delight as she toddled towards me. How I loved her! It was so good to see them again, and they all looked fine except my sister.

Margret had aged years within the last months and her face looked haggard and worn. How she kept going was beyond my understanding. Brave, ingenious woman! Three hungry little girls, fatherless—and somehow she managed to find a bit of flour, a loaf of bread, a cabbage head, some greens—something to eat every day. The children got most of it while she watched them eat. The only person who stood by her was Papa —our real father—the man I had hated all my life and whom I scarcely knew. He lived out in the country beyond the other end of the city. His Czech wife had a few goats and a garden. Though it was a long way out there, every so often my sister left her children and went to get a jug of milk for Uta from Papa.

Milk was as precious as gold, but my sister fixed milk soup for me because she knew of my ulcer pains. While I sipped the hot soup, feeling guilty for eating her children's food, we talked softly. There was no safety for me at her place; it was just a matter of time before my pursuers would find me. And the next time they would take me to a labour camp father east—oh, so much farther east! Siberia was cold, silent, and endless; there would be no way back a second time for me. My sister suggested that I stay just long enough to regain my strength before going on from there. But where would I go?

I slept and ate and slept again. My sister's meagre food supplies went fast with the extra mouth to feed, and we all knew it.

"Let me go out to Papa's place and see if I can get some milk and vegetables for you," I said one morning, feeling almost like myself again. My sister looked surprised.

"*You* want to go and see Papa?"

"Why not?" I asked defensively. "Regardless how I feel about him and that witch of a wife he is married to, it's time that we get better acquainted. Besides, I want to be of some help to you! As for being safe, I think I can manage. I doubt that anyone will take me in; they usually come at night to get people."

With two empty jugs hidden in a knapsack, I started out. I was hot and thirsty when at last I arrived at my father's place.

"Well, what gives me the honour of seeing my Nazi daughter?" he asked sarcastically. I swallowed hard. The few times our paths had crossed during the war had been just in the reverse. I had been the one who had treated him haughtily and with contempt. I knew he was against the Nazis, and in my eyes he had also stooped below his German dignity when he had married a Czech woman. Besides, I would never forgive him for having forsaken me.

I met his steel-grey eyes without blinking. "I came for Uta's sake, Herr Papa," I said. "She needs milk, and Grittli is not very strong any more."

Papa's eyes softened. I knew he loved his little grand-daughter, and my oldest sister was close to his heart. I handed him the knapsack.

From the bedroom came a scolding, high-pitched voice. "Who is out there, Robert? Don't you give any food away; we have scarcely enough for ourselves! Remember that everything here is mine! You wouldn't have it any more but that you're married to me, a Czech woman. Don't you dare!"

"What is the matter with her?" I said softly but with disgust.

Papa wrinkled his nose. "Oh, she is sick. Her meanness is slowly eating her guts out. I think she has cancer, but who knows?"

He stepped into the cool storage room and poured milk into the jugs and stuffed some potatoes, carrots and other vegetables into the knapsack without looking up. I watched him. Was he really that heartless, bitter stranger I imagined him to be? Was he really as proud and hard as I saw him?

He looked tall, grey, and bony. There were two deep lines around his thin, tight lips and his brows wrinkled in obvious anger because the petty voice in the bedroom still went on. I knew enough about him and his famous temper to wonder why she would suddenly dare to be so persistent in her quarrelling. I knew from hearsay that he had given her many a beating in years past. Oh, yes, suddenly she had become the master in the house, sick or not—for Papa wore a white band on his sleeve like I did—and she could throw him out of his house and keep everything. She could make him a beggar, a refugee like so many other Germans who had to leave day after day, kicked out by Czechs and pushed over the border with nothing but their stigma and the clothing on their backs.

Papa handed me the full knapsack and stood up. A deep premonition seized me that it was the last time we would see each other, and it melted some of my resentment.

"Papa," I said, "I will leave Margret's place soon and not bother you any more. But all my life I wanted to ask you one question: Why did you forsake your children when Mama died?" My bitterness came back and my mouth felt dry.

Papa looked me up and down as if he hadn't heard my question. "Girl, you look like your mother. Did you know that your mama was beautiful? The only thing, your hair isn't long like Maria's. Her braids came down to her knees. Oh, she was so good and sweet . . ."

Did I see tears in his eyes? Impossible! That rough old man wouldn't know how to cry.

"Papa," I said coldly, "I asked you a question; would you mind answering me before I leave? Our paths might never cross again and I might wonder forever. Papa, why did you leave us?" I blinked in unbelief. He did have tears in his eyes!

"*Marichen*, someday you will understand. You *are* my flesh and blood and we belong to each other regardless how you feel about me. I didn't want to confuse you, child. I couldn't get you. She . . ."—he frowned towards the bedroom—"wouldn't let me. I married her because she had hair like your mama's. But she didn't have anything else like her, and I've lived in hell ever since your mama died. She was my angel!"

I felt myself softening and resented it. "Papa, if my mama was so good, why did you treat her so mean? They say she died because of you!"

"Is that what those Christians told you about me?" Papa jerked as if a needle had pierced him. "I thought they were better than that!"

"Leave Christianity out of it, sir," I said defensively. "I believe in it as little as you do, but if it comes down to facts, they were good enough to keep me, weren't they?"

"Yes, child." Papa suddenly looked very tired. "They did, and you should always be grateful to them. Now go before she finds out that it is you. She might try to harm you!"

"*Auf Wiedersehen*," I said and shook his hand. I wanted to ask him for a glass of water, but my pride was greater than my thirst and I walked away without turning back to wave at him. I had every reason to despise him, and I was glad he went through hell with that bad woman. He deserved it, and it made me feel good. Or did it? All at once I felt very sad and alone.

My sister was very happy about the food and she cooked enough stew that evening to fill all of us up to our ears. It was a feast! I tried to forget that old, strange man called Papa and it wasn't too hard. I was too worried about myself to think very much about anyone else.

My head had been hazy since I had left that labour camp. Something was wrong with my mind—yes, with my memory. It worried me day and night. I felt like an animal in a cage. I was frightened most of the time. Whenever I tried to recall the past the fog closed in. In that fog I recognized familiar faces, places, people, but the names were gone. Names, where were all the names of the past? It had even haunted me while I had faced my Papa. I couldn't remember the name of that wretched woman who had struck from her bedroom at us—witch without name, did I care if I knew it?

I could have asked my sister. She knew that name and many other names I had lost. But I would never do that. What if she thought I was insane? Maybe I was! But not crazy enough to admit to her or to anyone else that my enemies had managed to crack me up! Not for the life of me. I was a German, a German of a lost, shattered, but great Reich. In my ear I could still hear my dead Fuhrer's voice: "They can break us but they can never bend us!"

If I had to go under I would go proudly with my head high, the way I had walked away from Herr Appelt, the man who begot me—the way I had left that miserable labour camp. Nobody would ever know that they had been able to get me down. Nobody! I hated them all.

Soon I had to make another decision. Not far from us lived a prosperous Czech family who had been friendly towards our family for a long time. The son of the family belonged to the National Guard. When he found out that I had returned to my sister's place, he visited us regularly, assuring us of his good intentions and even bringing us small amounts of bread and potatoes. I treated him politely, but laughed at my sister's suggestion that Vladislav was courting me.

I stopped laughing when our young neighbour came to see me one day and asked gravely if he might talk to me. I nodded politely, and we went for a walk. It was safe to leave the house with him beside me because his position protected me even though I wore my white armband. Vladislav, after stuttering for a while, announced that he had just received orders to bring me to the labour office in the city. I was horrified. Would he really do it?

He hesitated, then continued. "Manjo, there is not a thing you can do about it. Even if you hide, the militia will find you by and by. But—" and his round, simple face blushed as he continued, "there is one way out for you, and that is to marry a Czech man. It would change your status and you would be considered a free citizen of the Czech Republic. Well, and— and—since I feel real love in my heart for you, and since I am well able to start my own *domecku* (little home) for both of us, will you consider it?"

I looked into his red, sweaty face. Was Vladi aware of what he was doing? Other Czech men had dared to marry German girls within the last few months, and many more German girls were trying to make such contacts as an easy way out of a desperate situation. But with my young neighbour it was different! As a *narodny* (national Czech) his marriage with a German girl could endanger his future career.

I shook my head. "No, Vladi, that is not good for you and your future. I thank you for your willingness to save me from labour camp, but I cannot accept the offer!"

The young man was not easily convinced. He urged, pleaded, and threatened. After all, he had the power to take me to the officials! My mind raced. I had to have time to think.

Meekly I asked him if he would give me time to think it over. The proposal had come as a surprise to me, and I had to think about it first and ask my sister for advice.

Vladi nodded happily and smiled, relieved, and walked me back to my sister's home. Before I slipped through the door, he assured me again that not only my problems but my sister's would be over as soon as I gave my yes. Vladi would bring food for the children, and clothing, shoes—I nodded a friendly good night and went inside.

I could never marry that Czech man. I had not a spark of love for him in my heart, and I would never do what my papa had done. I had looked down on him ever since I had known him and I was prejudiced enough towards the Czechs as a whole that I would never join them. But I had no choice but to stall him. It was tempting to say, "Yes" and give up struggling, but I just couldn't do it. If nothing else, it would not be fair to him. I could not make him happy and I didn't want to, either!

In two days he would return from a patrol trip, so I lost no time. I didn't have much civilian clothing, but I hastily packed what little I did have, my dirndl, my only white knee socks, a sweater and some other small pieces of clothing in a knapsack, and my sister helped me to sew my few valuable possessions into the lining of my coat. The only document I took with me was my Catholic birth certificate. All my other important papers I laid in an airtight metal box and buried it in the backyard during the night. My report cards, diplomas, and other records were Nazi papers, signed and sealed with different stamps bearing the Nazi eagle and swastika. I didn't dare carry them on my flight from home.

Flight? Yes, I had to flee; but where? We knew that the "leftovers" of Germany had been divided. West Germany lay far to the west of us. Now East Germany had become a Communist republic, heavily occupied by Russian troops. West Germany was occupied by the Allies, mainly Americans. Rumour had it that the Americans were friendly. There was a ration card system, and people could buy food. Not much, of course, but enough to keep alive. The American soldiers, it was said, did not force their attentions on women; enough girls liked to be *Soldaten-Liebchen* (soldiers' sweethearts) so that the Americans left other people alone. This sounded too good to be true, and nobody knew anything for sure; but just in case those marvellous reports were true I would try to go there. If I made it and found things otherwise, I wouldn't have lost anything.

One night later I left for West Germany, but not alone. Micherle, one of my former dormitory mates from the Nazi school, wanted to join me, and I didn't have the heart to turn her down. Her parents had been taken to a labour camp, leaving her alone and helpless.

My sister's children had already gone to sleep when I bent sadly over Uta's small baby bed. I loved that child! Would I ever see her again? Would I ever see anybody again? My sister put a crust of bread into my knapsack and a few dried blueberries. I knew she had taken them from her own children.

We did not say much as I stepped out the back door. What was there to say? I looked once more over at Vladi's house.

Everything was dark. I wondered how he would feel when he returned the next day and found the bird flown. Would he become a real German-hater? I knew I was betraying his trust. Would he ever understand that I was doing the best for both of us? "Good-bye, Vladi. Good luck to you, and thanks for your kindness. May you forgive me that I chose freedom rather than a life of ease!"

We soon reached the borderline between Czechoslovakia and East Germany. Both parts were occupied by Russian troops and governed by Communists. Therefore the boundary was not carefully guarded, and we got across it unmolested.

We took off our white bands, which had marked us for so long as outcasts, for Germany did not require them. Then with new hope we began our long tramp through East Germany. Unfortunately, the weather seemed to turn against us and all the other refugees who milled around all over the country. It rained for hours, for days, for weeks. We moved on as in a nightmare with drenched clothing clinging to our bodies until a merciful sun shone for a few hours and dried us a little. Our hungry stomachs woke us up at night while we tried to sleep in the woods or hide in the ditches.

There were evenings when I was so exhausted and racked by pains from my ulcerated stomach that I felt tempted to give up. For food we had only a few herbs from the woods, wild berries, and roots. Did it make any sense to keep going? Oh, yes, there was Micherle, who had trusted her life into my hands when she had joined me in my long journey. She was younger than I and less independent. She had been rendered too soft by doting parents who were suddenly gone. If nothing else, I had to keep going for her sake.

At night, whenever we were lucky enough to find a fairly dry shelter to sleep under, we would dream of food—rich, appetizing, warm, tantalizing food. We eagerly reached for it only to wake up empty and cold. We talked about food, tried to remember how certain things tasted. We did not long for fancy stuff; just a bowl of soup, a good piece of bread, fresh boiled potatoes. But there was nobody to share with us—too many refugees on the roads. The farmers and villagers kept their homes locked, the barns barred, the orchards and fields guarded by dogs and traps.

My greatest trial was still my befuddled mind! My memory had not returned after many days, and I tormented myself for hours trying to force my brain to remember. The search for my mother's name obsessed me, but I could not find it regardless of how hard I tried.

One ray of light shone, one consolation, one hope. In the darkest hours of discouragement and despair, while cold, sleepless, and bent over with pain, I was able to close my eyes and think of Mother. I didn't know her name; I couldn't remember many incidents of my childhood, but I still could visualize her as a person. Whenever my heart called for her, she seemed to be there; and my vision of her was always, of all things, in the frame of evening worship!

There she sat at the window looking out towards the crimson evening sky or the dark clouds that towered above the hills. Her blue eyes would get a faraway look, then she would start to sing. Her voice was not fancy or full, but silvery like a child's voice. She would run out of breath before the end of the phrase was reached, because her heart was not strong and she was short of breath. She loved *"Näher mein Gott zu Dir"* (Nearer, My God, to Thee) and *"Oh bleibe Herr, der Abend bricht herein"* (Abide with Me), and we all joined in. After the singing, Father would reach for the family Bible and read a psalm.

Yes, Mother's worship hours stayed with me when everything else had left me. Her peaceful face bent towards me in the darkest hours of the night and my life, and I sensed that I had lost something great. Peace—mother's peace—I couldn't give it up, lie down, and die. I had to get up every new dawn, move my stiff limbs, grit my teeth, and go on tramping through the rain, searching for herbs or mushrooms to still that hurting stomach, and moving forward—always west—looking for what?

Mother, oh, Mother, where are you? Is there any peace and love left anywhere in this world?

After crossing the larger part of Thuringia, we arrived in a small village. Something was different in that village. What? The place was stuffed to the brim with refugees. They seemed to be everywhere, but only milling around, not moving west as they usually were.

"What's the matter?" A shrug, a sigh!

"*Niemandsland!*"

"What is that? No-man's-land?"

"Haven't you heard about that before?"

No, we hadn't. If we had, I would never have attempted to make my way west through all of East Germany, through long weeks of rain, starvation, fear and endless nights to a cruel strip of land several kilometres wide beyond the village, set up for one purpose only: to keep people, homeless, hungry, helpless people, from going across to West Germany. But why? What was over there Russians wouldn't want people to see?

I didn't dare to ask those questions aloud. I mingled with the crowds and just by listening I found out some hard facts all too soon. It was hopeless to try to make it across no-man's-land. Communist border guards patrolled the area heavily, twenty-four hours every day. The soldiers had orders to shoot at any moving object. There were some gruesome stories about people who had tried to cross it and had been shot, or caught and imprisoned.

It wasn't fair. It was so senseless. Why would the Russians try to keep the refugees in the *Arbeiter paradies* (labourer's paradise) when they didn't want them? There were thousands of people on the roads without food and shelter, and the Communists couldn't care less. But what was on the other side? Were Americans different? What form of government did they have? What would wait for us if we got across? According to my teachers in Prague, Americans were bloodsuckers like the British imperialists. Most puzzling of all, the Americans were allies of Russia and had helped them to beat Germany. Why would Russians now shoot people for trying to go over to their allies and friends? It was all so confusing. I couldn't even begin to figure it out and my head felt hazier than ever.

Dusk had settled over the village, and as the dripping fog rolled in from the river we shivered in our wet clothing. Clouds promised another heavy rain. Some windows lighted up behind drawn shades, suggesting warmth and a sense of belonging. How would it feel to sit near a big stone hearth and get warmed up again—warmed through and through?

On a sudden impulse, I walked up to a house and knocked! A weather-beaten sign told us that it had been a *Gasthaus* (guest house) in its better days, but naturally it was closed, for the *Gastwirt* (innkeeper) had nothing to offer any more. Yes, I knew it was senseless to knock, and Micherle's round eyes stared at me in surprise. Had I forgotten that doors did not open to people like us? People didn't bother any more even to look at the homeless, foodless, shelterless refugees who filled the roads. They didn't even bother to answer their knocking. But I knocked again, loud and eager, with determination.

Unexpectedly the door opened, and I looked into the kind eye of an elderly man. "What do you want?" he asked hesitatingly.

"Sir," I stammered, "we are so cold and soaked by the rain, we wondered if we could sit for a while beside your hearth to get dry?"

He looked at us, two strange girls with their clothes drip-

8

ping, the water squeezing in the old torn shoes—he must slam the door in our faces, and we would walk sadly into the night again.

"Well, come on in," said the man. "You poor girls!"

Had I heard right? The man was inviting us in?

With a humble "*Danke*" we stepped into the house, took off our shoes so we would not dirty the floor, and sat down by the hearth to dry our clothing. Oh, how good it felt to be warm! If we didn't disturb anyone maybe we could sit by the hearth until the people retired?

After a while the man came towards us with two steaming bowls of soup in his hands. Smiling, he asked us whether we wanted to eat some soup! Our hands trembled as we reached out for the bowls. We thanked the kind man over and over again.

Gratefully we handed back the empty bowls and spoons and sat quietly, waiting for the word that would send us out again into the stormy night. I felt a strong desire to talk to that friendly man about our plans to cross the border into the West. But it might prove disastrous. Still, this man had been so kind. Would he turn around and betray us if we asked for advice?

Time ticked away at the old cuckoo clock, and I knew I had to hurry. I threw my hair back over my shoulders with a determined head shake and said, "Sir, may I ask you a question?"

The man nodded.

"I don't have to tell you that we are refugees. We left my homeland, Czechoslovakia, weeks ago. We came west to cross the border, but we did not know about this no-man's-land. Sir, we've got to get across it, but we don't know how. Do you have a map of this area so we could find a way? We would like to cross tonight."

The man began to laugh. No, not malicious—it sounded

like a friendly, amused laugh. But why would a man laugh under such circumstances?

"You naive little things!" he said. "You sound like a dog barking at the moon. How can you think of crossing the countryside with only a map? No, no, girls! Soldiers are out there day and night to catch you. You couldn't possibly make it."

"But, sir," I pleaded, "isn't there any way at all? I've got to leave because I escaped from a labour camp. If I stay here they will find me and put me back into one of those horrid camps."

"Yes," he finally answered, "there is one pass yet where Germans are going across, but the way is very hard to find. Only a guide can lead you through, and"—his voice became a whisper—"there is such a guide in the village. It's the ferryman down at the river. If you can pay him enough he may take you, but he is asking a lot. He wants watches, jewellery—"

I interrupted him excitedly. "Sir, we have a few things hidden in the lining of our clothing. Maybe it will be enough to please him. At least we can try. Oh, thank you, sir, for being so kind and open towards us. I do not know how I ever can repay you, but let me assure you of our deepest appreciation!"

The man nodded, rose from his chair, and said simply, "You girls may sleep in our house tonight. Not even a dog should be out on a night like this, and you girls look as if you need some rest. Tomorrow you can see the ferryman."

He led us upstairs to a room with two beds. The cover on each bed was a bulging featherbed, and there were soft pillows. He bade us good night and left.

We looked at each other, dumbfounded. We must be dreaming! People like that man didn't really exist! The beds felt real, and though the raindrops drummed on the small window, no rain was hitting us.

Before we retired, we ripped certain parts of our clothing open and laid our treasures out in a little pile. It wasn't a fortune, but the things seemed valuable enough to make a try the next morning. The only thing I hated to lose was a silver bracelet Rudy had sent me. A piece of my heart went along with it. Another thing I had treasured was my colourful silk scarf. It made a bright little bundle after we had tied our valuables in it. Then we eagerly slipped under the soft feather covers. We felt guilty to be sleeping so comfortably, for we knew how many of our fellow refugees were out in the rain.

During the night I awakened several times with a feeling of dread. "Maybe we're in a trap," I thought. "When will somebody come in and order us out? Surely we cannot sleep a whole night in a soft, warm bed!"

Nobody came to chase us out. When morning came, I awakened Micherle because we had to go and find the ferryman. She was not happy about rising early; who knew when we might sleep in a real bed again?

Careful not to disturb our kind host's family, we tiptoed out of the house and stepped into a dull grey morning. For the first time in days our clothing was dry, and we felt warm and rested. In our hearts we felt a new hope. The happenings of the last evening seemed like a good omen.

We found the river dirty with yellow-brown mud, and swiftly flowing as a result of continuing rain. We waited at the wharf, and I felt a pang of fear when the ferry appeared. What if the man said no? What if he asked for more pay? We had nothing more to give!

With a forced cheery, "Good morning," we stepped on the raft and paid our fee. The man steered quietly across, gazing silently into the water. We were the only passengers, and as we reached the middle of the river, I took a deep breath and began my speech.

"Sir," I said, "somebody has told us that you are a guide who will take refugees across the border if the pay is equal to the chance you are taking. Now, sir"—I talked in haste so he would not interrupt until I had finished—"I do not know whether our valuable things we brought with us will be enough, but look and see." Hastily I untied my bundle and laid it at his feet.

"No. I don't do such things. You know that the Russians would shoot me if they caught me doing that!"

I nodded emphatically. "Yes, I know, but look. We *must* get across. Believe me, we are not spies. We have come from Czechoslovakia and have walked a long, long way. Please help us! I escaped from a labour camp, so I ran away and my girl-friend with me. Is it not enough that we offer you? Look at it, sir. It's all we have to give, friend. We hold nothing back. Won't you take us?"

He stared at my bundle and remained silent for what seemed a long time. At last he nodded his unkempt head and said, "Ja, girls, I will take you tonight. I shall meet you half an hour before midnight, over there," and he pointed towards the hills where the evergreen woods spread. "Where the woods begin you will find a small trail leading into the underbrush. Stand behind trees till I come."

Jubilantly I pressed his hand and thanked him profoundly. Then I asked him to take the ferry back, for we had no reason to cross to the other side. Our mission had been accomplished.

## 10
## Escape

Time dragged by as we wandered aimlessly around. We must not draw attention to ourselves. The less a person was noticed by the soldiers, the better. As soon as it was dark enough we made our way to the woods. We knew we would have to wait, but we wanted to find the assigned meeting place. Undisturbed, we crossed fields and meadows and after some searching found the brush trail. We stepped under the trees and waited. After a while we noticed that we were not alone. Many silent figures stood under dripping trees as we did and waited. I whispered, "How will the man take such a large group across without being detected?" Micherle shrugged her shoulders.

We had another worry on our minds. Would the guide really come? What if he didn't? We had given him all we owned. What if he betrayed us after collecting our stuff?

More people arrived, among them women and children, even babies. The night was dark and foggy and it drizzled. How did those mothers keep their little ones from protesting loudly about the unearthly hour and the cold rain? Maybe the guide had advised the mothers what to do, for all the babies had nappies tied around their mouths, with their noses left open for breathing. This muffled their little voices sufficiently for safety. Pre-school children held tightly to their mothers' hands or skirts, not daring to whisper or cough.

What a relief when the guide finally appeared! He whispered orders, and the group lined up in single file. Information from the front would be given by signs, which were to be passed on from one person to the next. He briefly explained the route and some landmarks that marked the border over which we would have to run. Then the silent figures began to move forward, led by that rough-looking man who was willing to risk his life either for the pay he received or because he felt called to help. I didn't know why, and it didn't matter as long as he was doing it.

Our progress was slow because every step had to be cautious and noiseless. Flashlights could not be used (most of us did not own such a luxury, anyway), and the guide led us part of the way through dense underbrush where it was hard, especially for the mothers with children, to move without noise. Micherle and I were near the rear, while the mothers with children were in the middle of the line so we could give a hand once in a while. We had already walked for a long, long time and I wondered if these woods would ever come to an end. The darkness had become pitch black and from previous sleepless nights I had learned that the darkest hour was always before morning dawn.

Dawn was again just below the horizon and I knew it. Any other night I had longed for morning to come but now I wished for darkness to stay. Stay, night, oh, stay! Cover us, night, hide us!

I turned my head back more often. Stumbling forward I ran into trees, barely feeling the pain because I was filled with panic. If the morning light was faster than we, the Russians would see us, for the most dangerous part of our journey was still ahead.

I turned my head again, and there it was—that first nudge

of morning dawn touching the black tops of the many trees behind me with dark grey mist. Fear grabbed me and took my breath away. Then, oh, what a relief, there was finally the sign I had waited for, the sign which indicated that the Russian patrol line was only metres away. Now we were again on our own because here the ferryman had to leave us to make his way back. Now each of us would try to break through the brush to cross the border line. Micherle stood close to me waiting for my signal to run.

Suddenly we heard Russian guards shouting, "*Stoj! Stoj! Stoj* (stop)!" Next we heard shots followed by screams and then soldiers cursing and shouting. I threw myself flat on the muddy ground behind a bush, and Micherle lay close beside me, breathing heavily. The wood had opened its merciful arms and swallowed us up; we saw none of the others of our group. The shooting stopped, and all was silent again. Only our hearts beat so loudly that we felt the ground would transmit the sound to the enemy soldiers.

My thoughts raced: "Maria Anne, dumb girl, you ran into a trap. The Russians are in front of us. Shall we turn back?" Impossible! Morning was breaking, and we could never make it back through no-man's-land without being caught. This must be the end.

Suddenly we heard a child screaming. It was not far from us, calling for its mother. Dear me, why didn't those mothers watch their children better in an hour like this? This child would attract the soldiers. I worked my way towards the child, remaining flat on the ground while moving forward on my elbows and slightly bent knees.

The child was a skinny, frightened little girl, three or four years old, with blonde, wet strands of hair hanging over her shoulders. I closed her mouth tightly with my hand and whispered, "Be quiet, child! The Russians will find us if you scream so loud. Where is your mother?"

I took my hand from her mouth so she could talk. She sobbed softly as she told me that her mother had held her baby brother in one arm while she, the "big sister", had held Mother's other hand. When the shooting began, *Mammi* was suddenly gone and "big sister" found herself alone in the big dark woods.

"If you stop crying, honey, we shall see if we can't find *Mammi* somewhere. Come with me over to where my girl friend is waiting." I stroked her head and wiped her tears away, and we crawled cautiously back to Micherle.

Time was running out. Morning was moving in fast, and time would work against us if we didn't hurry. I looked at the strange child who had cuddled up with childlike confidence, trusting me to find her mother. We would have to run somewhere, but how could we run if we kept the child with us? On the other hand, could we leave her alone in the woods and run away?

"Listen, we will try to make it across the border," I decided. "We cannot go back, and we will be caught for sure here in no-man's-land. We must try for the American Zone."

I turned to the child. "*Häschen* (little rabbit), we will take you along. Maybe your mother made it across, and we will find her over there. Now you must promise two things: you must run as fast as your little feet will carry you, and you must not make any noise. Do you think you can do that for me?"

The girl nodded gravely, without a word. She had already begun to keep her promise.

I showed Micherle how to get a fast grip on the child's hand without hurting her wrist in case we had to pull her, then I took the child's other hand securely, and we began to run.

First we ran down the last metres to the foot of the wooded hill. Then we had to cross a small road running through the valley, which was the actual patrol line of the Eastern guards. After crossing a deep ditch by the road we entered an open grassy area without trees or bushes to protect us. We ran in desperation, expecting bullets to hit us any moment. At the meadow's end we came to a small creek whose waters looked swift and murky from the rains. We had no chance to guess the depth of the creek. We waded into the swift water and splashed across as fast as we could. Stumbling and struggling, our main concern was to keep the child's head above the water and keep our balance. As we struggled ashore at the other side, ice-cold water ran in little streams down our hips and legs, and our coats clung heavily to us. We reached some woods again and started running uphill. We knew that the American patrol line was at the top of the hill.

Partway up, I threw myself down in exhaustion. "I have to rest awhile," I gasped. "I can't go on another step even if the Russians are after us." Micherle had laid down too, breathing in short, sharp gasps.

Why hadn't the Russians shot at us? I wondered. We had been perfect targets. Why did we get through unmolested? I could think of no answer. Did the soldiers see us and take pity on the little child between us? Soldiers may be cruel when drunk, but perhaps they have tender hearts when sober. Most of them love children. I had seen Russians share their lunches with hollow-cheeked, begging children more than once. Maybe the officer in charge was a father himself and hadn't been able to shoot when he saw those little legs running in desperation!

My eyes fell upon the child. For a moment I had forgotten her! There she stood, dripping wet from neck to water-filled shoes. Her little body shook, and her teeth chattered. Tears rolled down her cheeks, drawing straight lines on the mud-smeared face. But no loud sob escaped her blue lips; she wept noiselessly and waited without complaint. Why must little tots suffer so much? I wondered.

"Quick, Micherle, pull something out of my knapsack.

There should be something dry on top. We must change the child's coat or she will catch pneumonia for sure." Hastily I pulled off the child's dripping coat and wrapped her in my dry sweater.

Overtired, she snuggled herself trustingly on my shoulders. What else could I do but pick her up and carry her? Micherle put my knapsack over one of my shoulders and then we began to climb the hill again. The child fell asleep, and with the extra load I had to use all my will power to keep going. One step, one more, one again—will the top of the hill never come? What if the soldiers should catch us just a few metres short of the goal? "Don't think, Maria, just keep going!"

I struggled on to climb some more of the steep slope, but the mountain had vanished. I walked on and lifted my foot. How come the ground was even? Where had the hill gone? Some thought seemed to try to dig into my skull, but my temples throbbed from exhaustion and fear. Keep going. Keep going. Don't stop. You are saved. Go—stop—run! No, you made it! Thoughts at war, but my feet were too tired to walk anymore, and suddenly we had arrived! I finally believed myself and laid the child down for a moment and turned to look eastward. The dark evergreens stretched away for miles, and somewhere in those dark woods were my pursuers. Death and I had met again, and I had been spared. Why?

I bent over and looked into the child's white face. Her closed eyelids flickered, and shivers shook the undernourished little form. Gently I lifted her from the damp ground and turned to the west. I knew I had to find help fast if that child were to survive, and I was determined to find it. In the distance blinked a light.

"Let's go towards the light," I urged. "Maybe somebody will take the child in."

Steadying ourselves, we lifted the child and began to walk again, across fields and pastures, over rocks and little streams.

The light came nearer while the dawn yielded to a new day.

But maybe I was just dreaming. Maybe I just thought that a new day was beginning. Maybe it was dark, would stay dark, for ever and ever—and more darkness was ahead of me. I had wished for it! I was afraid! I had escaped the Russians, yes, but would the Americans be any better? And the light in the sky, was it morning or evening? Did I really hear a lark above me? Was there anyone I could trust? Was light stronger than darkness? Would I wake up someday and know that everything had only been a horrible nightmare? Would there ever be a new morning for me?

# II

## From America, with Love

If I hadn't been so tired I would have noticed it: as we approached the building with the light, it did not register on our minds that the building was not a German farmhouse. I only knew I couldn't carry that child another step, and that the child was deathly pale.

I stepped up to the door and knocked. No reply. I started to beat the door with my fist, determined not to let up until somebody answered. Maybe if the farm family could see the child, they might be willing to help. All I wanted was a warm place where the child might get dry.

Unexpectedly the door opened, and there stood an American soldier. I knew he was an American. I had seen pictures of such soldiers during the war while I trained as a Nazi. I didn't remember much that I had been taught about those men; only two things: American men, living in big dirty cities, were all shooting gangsters; and they chewed gum, which was a teeth-destroying habit.

The soldier before me stood tall, armed—and chewing! "What do you want?" he drawled, moving his gum from one side to the other while his teeth gleamed at me.

I was petrified with fear, and my scared face must have

spoken louder than my German words as I stuttered and mumbled my plea. I knew no English at all, and obviously the soldier did not understand my German. He gave me a puzzled look, then turned and called a name. Presently an interpreter appeared and asked me in German what we wanted.

"We just crossed over from the Russian side, and we found this child alone in the woods," I explained. "We had to cross the river and the child got soaked up to her head. She will die unless we can get her warm and dry. And please tell that soldier that he should not send us back to the Russians—' The child had buried her face on my shoulder and sobbed silently.

The next thing that happened I had never thought possible, not even in my dreams and imaginations. The door opened wide and we were invited in! Other soldiers appeared and brought a cot and blankets. They told me to wrap a blanket around the child and remove her wet clothing. Then we laid the cold little form on the cot. Meanwhile, another soldier had brought a big cup of hot chocolate. As I lifted the child's head up, she sipped the drink eagerly and greedily. Slowly I watched the colour come back into her face, and her cold hands loosened their tight grip on my fingers. Gently I put her head back and told her to go to sleep. She nodded, and I stepped back into the corner where Micherle stood.

But some of the soldiers began to talk to the child. It was a strange language, to be sure, but it sounded as if they were trying to talk baby talk. They made funny faces and rolled their eyes like clowns. She sat up and watched. After a while she had lost her shyness and talked happily with those strange, big boys. They had a merry time together in spite of the fact that they could not understand each other's words.

I stood in my corner and watched, mystified. How could this all be true? Through ignorance, we had run into a situation where we were at the mercy of American soldiers, our enemies. They had taken us in and helped the child; now they were entertaining her, laughing and jumping. Why would gangsters, who hated the Germans so badly that they had come across the ocean to fight us, treat us so kindly? This had to be a big trap, but it didn't look like a trap. It seemed so real! Did I dare to think that Americans were not gangsters, just friendly human beings? Maybe I had been misinformed. Again I had the feeling that something was breaking within me. Yes, my previous concept of American people was crumbling. Goebbel's hateful propaganda was proving to be lies again.

At last the little girl fell asleep, and the soldiers became quiet. Some had tiptoed away, and the others stood beside the cot. I stepped forward and looked down at the resting child. Well, we had accomplished what we had tried to do, and it was time for Micherle and me to leave again. The child seemed to be in good hands. I nodded a shy *Danke* and made for the door.

Before I reached it, a soldier spoke up. He motioned and tried to make me understand something. He rubbed his eyes and asked, "Are you tired, sleepy—you want to sleep too?"

So that was it! Soldiers were all alike, I thought. I shook my head in disgust and backed towards the door. "*Nein, nein, Danke,*" I whispered hoarsely.

The soldier seemed to read my thoughts. "Look," he said proudly, and pointed towards himself, "I American." His big chest seemed to widen several centimetres! He spoke slowly and deliberately, and I nodded. I understood. Yes, he was an American!

"I no Russian." He pointed towards the east and shook his head emphatically.

I nodded again. No, he was not a Russian!

"I good man." *Guter Mann* in German—it sounded similar enough to me that I got the meaning. I thought I understood and nodded hesitatingly. He grinned and showed his big white teeth.

I stared at him. Was he really good? Each of us knew what the other was thinking.

He went to a door, opened it, and motioned us to enter. We saw two cots with blankets in a small room. Most likely it was one of their first-aid rooms. He nodded, gestured, and rubbed his eyes again. "You sleepy, go rest. We—good men."

I hesitated again. It was against common sense to trust, and I knew it was better to turn and run. But somehow I couldn't! Those cots looked so good, the blankets so dry and warm, and my eyes were so heavy. I had been running away from everything for many weeks. I was so tired of running. Yes, I would take a chance and lie down and sleep while all those soldiers swarmed around. It was foolish to trust, but I would do it anyway.

With a trace of a smile I looked into the eyes of our host and nodded slowly. Politely he held the door open and ushered us in, then he closed the door carefully and was gone. Without further delay we threw ourselves onto those cots and spread the blankets over us. We went to sleep within minutes.

I do not know how long we had slept when a loud knock on the door made me jump. Frightened, I called, "Who is it? What do you want?"

In stepped a soldier in white, who proved to be an American army cook. His face was round, full, and pink. He looked healthy and pleasant. He smiled broadly, and that made his face rounder and fuller still. A high white cap towered over his head. At the middle he seemed to be round and full also; a white apron covered a lot of waist. In his arms he carried a tray loaded with food. He put the tray down and asked with a jolly wink, "You want to eat?"

Hardly believing my ears and eyes, I nodded. We were supposed to eat something! I looked at the tray. It was loaded with food. I wondered which of all these things we would be permitted to eat. Obviously the man would eat with us. I looked into his face and waited for him to give further orders.

"Eat," he urged again, as we hesitated.

"*Alles* (all of it)?" I asked breathlessly.

"Yeah, all." He seemed amused.

"*Danke! Danke!*"

He grinned and left the room.

Our hands shook as we reached for the food. I tried to butter my bread. I had never seen snow-white bread before; the rye bread of my country had been dark and coarse. White baked goods were called *Kuchen* (cake). Why, I wondered, would American soldiers begin their day eating cake with butter and jelly, besides all the other things, some of them strange to us, just for a simple meal like breakfast! Puzzling or not, this food was tastier and fancier than anything we had eaten for many weeks, and there was so much! We also had pots of steaming coffee. It was a new taste. I had only known grain coffee before, and the new taste was tangy and bitter. But it was a drink, anyway, and it warmed us inside. When we picked up the last few crumbs, we wiped our mouths with paper napkins. What a luxury! Napkins! Unheard of in postwar Germany. Maybe we were only imagining things!

We stretched out on the cots and tried to sleep again. The cook had come in to take the empty tray away and had motioned that we should go back to sleep. But sleep would not come, and I felt disgusted with myself. To have a chance to sleep for a few hours under real covers, in a real house, and then to lie awake! I didn't know much about coffee then.

"Let's get up," I finally suggested, so we did. We folded the blankets neatly and fished through our knapsacks for some dry clothing. Our skirts were still damp and terribly wrinkled, so we changed into our *Dirndls*, typical German garments of

9

pleated wide skirts with white blouses and special bodices. We put white socks on and brushed our tangled hair long and carefully. We felt like new people! Stepping out into the hall, we looked around to find somebody we could·say our *Danke* to once more before leaving.

The interpreter asked us to come into the office. The officer in charge greeted us with a polite nod of his grey head, and spoke rapidly. Then the interpreter said in German, "The lieutenant has contacted the Russian headquarters across the border to get some information about the child you brought in. The Russians knew about the lost child, for they caught the mother with the baby. We offered to return the child to the Russian border so it could be given back to its mother, but the Russians refused to take her back, in order to punish the mother.

"We cannot keep the little girl with us here in the barracks," the interpreter continued apologetically. "It's not the right place for her. Our office has contacted the International Red Cross in the next village. They have promised to take care of the child. Will you kindly take her to the next village and deliver her to the Red Cross lady there?"

The little girl was brought in. Somebody had been kind enough to wash and comb her hair, and her clothing was dry. She smiled radiantly and showed us her new possessions. Her pockets were filled with candies, crackers—and gum! Oh dear! After another thank you, we took the child's hand and started to leave. As we walked towards the entrance, somebody called once more. The interpreter told us, "The lieutenant said you should go right away to the office window at the Red Cross station; don't stand in line!"

"Yes, thank you," I answered. I didn't know what he meant.

As we walked away from the barracks I looked back and saw a scene I will never forget. Out of every window and door looked smiling GI faces, arms were waving and words we couldn't understand reached our ears.

I was completely mystified. Up to the last moment I had expected trouble. Now we walked away and the enemy soldiers waved after us without stopping us. They seemed to have a great time, laughing, joking—what was it that made Americans so different?

"*Danke,*" I said, "*danke schön, danke.*" I knew no English, I couldn't say what I felt. I couldn't ask any questions. I walked away and wondered—wondered why those men had been so kind to us.

I understood the advice of the lieutenant, however, after we arrived in the village an hour later and found the Red Cross refugee office. People stood in line for blocks! I remembered the parting words of the German interpreter and marched boldly by the long rows of refugees, who watched us with critical eyes.

Before anybody could stop me, I said, "Please, madam, an American officer said I should come right away up to your window and bring you this little girl because—"

"Come right in," said the uniformed lady, opening the door. In we marched, while hundreds looked on and perhaps silently protested.

"Sit down," encouraged the nurse, and settled herself behind the desk.

What was happening all around us? Refugess were not treated like this. Nobody had bothered to offer us a chair or food or shelter for so long. Suddenly everybody seemed to be kind. First, the Americans giving us food and sleep, now the lady with the Swiss accent treating us like people. All these foreign people seemed to be so human.

"You girls," she said smilingly; "the American lieutenant told me over the telephone about you and the child. I want you to know that we respect you highly for saving the child while you were running for your lives. It was wonderful of you to take her with you."

"*Schwester*," (nurses in Germany are called "sister") I answered, embarrassed, "we didn't do anything special. I mean, we couldn't have left the little thing all alone in the dark woods, could we?"

"No, dear, you couldn't have left her in the woods, but many would have left her. We are glad that you didn't."

I smiled down at my little friend. As usual, she held tightly on to my hand or skirt and seemed to be content as long as she could stay near me. I stroked her hair while she cuddled close.

The lady continued. "We have a little problem, girls. The International Red Cross office in the next large city is trying to make arrangements for the child, but every *Heim* (emergency shelter for refugee children) is overfilled; no bed available. It will take a few days to make room somewhere for your little foundling, and I am wondering if you two girls would be willing to care for her until we find a place."

"But *Schwester*," I interrupted, "we are more than willing to do so, only we have absolutely nothing for her! We gave all our valuable things to the guide who led us across no-man's-land. We have no food, no shelter, no clothing for the child, nothing. I can keep her by my side, but I can't give any care."

"Oh, I forgot to mention," the nurse interrupted gently, "that the Red Cross will provide what is needed. We will register you."

She reached for her fountain pen and some forms. "We will give all three of you ration cards for a week and some money, and I will call the hotel and tell them to give you shelter until we call you again."

Had I heard right? That woman offered us a hotel room, food, and money just because we would baby-sit a little refugee? After filling out some information blanks, she reached for the telephone and reserved a room in the only hotel in the village, which had been taken over by the occupation army. We received ration cards and money and left the office.

When we stepped out, several refugees who stood in line surrounded us and asked eager questions. "How come you girls got to go in without waiting?" asked a haggard, tired-looking woman. She was trying to keep order among her children, who fussed and kicked around her. I told the story briefly.

"How lucky can somebody be?" said one man. "Do you realize that it usually takes people eight to ten days to register, be approved, and get a ration card? And here you girls crossed the border just last night and are all taken care of already!" We smiled apologetically and left in a hurry. We had no longing to get tangled up with long lines of people who couldn't help resenting our streak of luck.

We walked to the hotel and found our room with beds ready. I put the little girl down for a nap and sat beside her until she went to sleep. So we had tried to help a lost child! All at once that child had become our talisman. How strange! We had not saved her because we expected any reward, but it seemed almost as if life was rewarding us for the deed. Kindness, I thought, must beget kindness, and hate will beget hate. Every thought, every action brings forth after its kind.

For three days and nights we enjoyed the comfort of the hotel room. We used our ration cards and the money sparingly, but we slept a great deal and felt refreshed and rested. On the third day the Red Cross sent a message. A place had been secured, and we had to bring the child back to the Red Cross office. I did so with mixed feelings. We had become attached to each other, and the child didn't want to leave me. Furthermore, I did not want to give her up. But we had to be glad that she would be taken care of, and I tried to comfort her. Tears flowed freely as we hurried away. The last sound we heard was of the nurse trying to still the girl's screaming.

I never again heard of the child. Though I forgot her name,

I often thought of her and wondered what might have become of her. Did she ever rejoin her mother? Did her soldier daddy ever come back from the war? Only eternity will give me the answers, so I must wait.

## 12
## *Rudy!*

Following the country road to the southwest, we wandered along without plans. After all, we had made it, we had arrived in the West. We had refugee registration cards which assured us we could request another ration card every ten days, and even though this meant only a minimum of food, this would protect us from starvation.

What to do next? For weeks we had been urged on by one goal only—the West. Now that we had made it, we felt like boats without rudders. We began to drift. We walked slowly, passed many other refugees on every road, entered villages, and learned little tricks to make the ration cards last longer.

We saw unmistakable signs of new beginnings. In different places the people in the villages had already begun to rebuild. Children, women, and old men were busy among ruins, carrying rubbish away, scraping old bricks for reuse, mixing clay and straw for new bricks. Some stores had reopened to supply the few needs which could be supplied. Some restaurants were beginning to serve food to the milling refugees if they had ration cards and money. Every so often we treated ourselves extravagantly and bought a bowl of hot soup, though this took a big section out of our ration cards. Some drugstores had reopened, too, and tried to do business with almost nothing. They offered herbs and a limited supply of medicine to distribute for real emergencies. These supplies came from the occupation army. They also had worthless knicknacks on display for the eager refugees. It was almost an obsession with some of the homeless wanderers like us; they had to buy everything which was "free"—in other words without ration cards. It had become a habit for people to stroll through every drugstore looking eagerly for "free" merchandise. Once we were lucky enough to find a store where they sold cough drops without prescription. The stuff tasted horrible, but what did it matter? They filled the stomach for a while.

We arrived at Vohenstrauss, a fair-sized village not damaged by the war. As we wandered along the main street, we discovered a pharmacy. The urge was irresistible, as usual, to go in and try our luck. We kept our money supply up by selling part of our ration cards to people with more means, so we always had enough money. As we entered the dim old place, we noticed another young woman standing at the counter, talking to the white-haired pharmacist. Obviously they knew each other. Those villagers, we thought, had the advantage. They knew the people behind the counters and were favoured over strangers. Well, that was life!

Micherle and I looked around and searched. Any offerings which would be of any use to us? Nothing we could see. Well, we could ask for cough drops. We approached the man and asked politely for them.

At the sound of my voice the young woman looked up in surprise and stared at me. I stared back into two surprised brown eyes. I had seen that person before!

"Annemarie! What in the world are you doing here?"

It was Rudy's sister! We had not heard from each other since I had returned my ring to their mother, and I had often wondered what had become of her. I only knew that the Russians and Poles had taken over her province, Silesia.

Annemarie stretched her hands out, and I took them in mine. She was not able to talk at once, as tears brimmed in her eyes. We walked out of the building, Annemarie leading the way. Little by little we began to piece our stories together. Annemarie cried while she talked. My resentment began to melt as I listened. She and her parents had lost everything; they had saved nothing but their lives. Her father had caught pneumonia and had been near death for weeks. His wife had nursed him day and night. Food had been scarce and the valuable things they had carried had to be traded for milk and medicine.

"Maria Anne," sobbed Annemarie, "you wouldn't recognize Mother any more! She lost sixty pounds in six weeks. Father still looks like a shadow; he is so thin and pale, and he cannot climb stairs. We live out in the country because a kind woman opened her house to us and gave us an upstairs room. We are luckier than many because we have a roof over our heads and a bed for Father!"

For a moment I had to fight "it-serves-you-right" feelings. Then I felt ashamed of even thinking such thoughts. There was no need to feel good because Rudy's rich family had suddenly become poor, and we were all in the same boat. Deepest pity filled me as I looked at Annemarie. She had been a sheltered, over-protected girl, and not even the war had inconvenienced her too severely during the first four years. I tried to picture her fright and agony when they had fled from home. She looked so skinny and forlorn as she walked beside me pushing her landlady's bicycle.

'Annemarie," I said, "please take my heartiest greetings to your parents. Tell them that I have nothing against them anymore and that I wish you all the best of luck." Swallowing my pride with great effort, I added, "and, Annemarie, may I ask you how your brother is?"

"Oh, Maria Anne, don't you know?" Her eyes overflowed again. "Rudy is—dead for all we know." She proceeded to tell me why they thought so—lost boat, no mail for months.

Rudy dead? Yes, I had hoped he would be, because it was too hard to think he might be suffering in a prisoner-of-war camp. But now that I heard his sister say so, I knew that I had lied to my heart. No, I didn't want him to be dead! Life had become almost hopeful again since I had crossed over to West Germany, and I had to admit to myself that I had looked for him constantly ever since I had escaped my persecutors. I had studied lists of registered names in every Red Cross station. I had looked in every man's face in the hope of finding Rudy among the refugees. I had really begun to hope again because my heart refused to give up. My buried love had pushed and inspired me to wander on, to search, to find—to find *him*.

I had to be alone for a few moments because I was too proud to show how much I cared. Stopping, I tried to smile at Annemarie while I said: "Annemarie, I think Micherle and I should go back to town and let you bicycle home, or your mum might be worried. It was so good to see you again, and please do not forget to tell your mother I have no bitterness in my heart towards her. It is the least we all can do for Rudy, to make peace and forget the past."

Annemarie and I shook hands, and we parted. Micherle walked silently with me back to the village.

Rudy was dead, most likely. Again that cruel bit of hope that can keep people in agony for years preyed on my mind. What did it really matter? He wasn't mine anymore even if he still lived. A wave of despair and hopelessness swept over me. Was it worthwhile to keep going even here in the West? It was almost more than my pride could bear to realize my main purpose in going on had been my hidden hope to find Rudy.

A familiar voice called me. I turned around. In the distance I saw a girlish figure on a bicycle pushing the pedals as hard as she could while waving her hand and calling. It was Annemarie coming after us at top speed. Breathless, she pulled up to where we stood. "Maria Anne," she pleaded, "my mother would like to see you. As soon as I told her, she sent me right back after you. Please come and visit my parents."

Now I felt resentful. It was one thing to send a kind message —but it was another to go and see her, shake her hand, talk to her. What if I said the wrong thing? How far could I go in forgiving her before my hurt pride would take over? What if I tried to get even with her for her heartlessness in breaking us up?

My face must have shown my struggle, for Annemarie said softly, while her eyes pleaded, "Please, Marianne, come with me. Mother has changed, and if she wronged you, she has paid for it in more ways than one. You don't know how much it would mean to her to see you. Please, for Rudy's sake, come!"

I felt ashamed of myself. Surely I would go and see those two poor old people if they wanted me to. Why should I add to their sorrow by refusing? We turned again and walked with Rudy's sister until we reached a small village surrounded by hills and woods. Steeling myself, I climbed some stairs to their place. Seconds later I stood before two people whom I hardly recognied. Though hardly able to hide my shock at their appearance, I ran towards the mother and put my arms around her. She could not speak for a while, as she and the father began to cry. She seemed to know what I was thinking and tried to smile. "Yes, my girl, I know we have changed. Life has dealt hard with all of us. Come and sit down!"

She had food ready for us, bless her heart, and the old Silesian hospitality! She had gone to the landlady and asked for two eggs. That took a lot of courage. Some bread was ready also.

I could hardly eat, for I knew that they needed the food for themselves. The father was blue-lipped and short of breath and cried every time he began to talk. My last feeling of resentment melted in pity. Rudy's name was scarcely mentioned. Neither side felt free to talk about him.

As we got up to leave, the mother squeezed my hand. "Maria Anne," she said sadly, "I didn't mean to hurt you and I did not know that my boy loved you so deeply. He tried to find you again, but you never answered!"

"Let's forget the past," I said quietly, "and be friends again. Even if Rudy were still alive, he and I would never be able to get together again for marriage, but I would like to be friends with you for the rest of my life."

"Please, my girl, write as soon as mail will go again and you have a regular address, for you might be all Rudy left us, if he is dead." The father's blue lips quivered.

I nodded. "I will write to you," I promised, and kissed all three good-bye. Micherle and I climbed down the stairs and stepped out into the evening. Micherle, shy with strangers, hadn't said much, but as soon as we were alone, she started to chatter. The food had excited her the most. To think that we each had eaten an egg, fried! We had forgotten how good eggs tasted. What nice people!

That night we found a barn in the fields and slipped in for the night. The next morning I knew that the time had come to make a decision. "Micherle," I said, "this lingering around is no good for us. I think we should leave this area and tramp to the south. All my life I've longed to see the Alps. Let's go and see southern Bavaria."

"Let's go!" said Micherle excitedly. After several days of walking, and after hitching part of the way on some freight trains, we neared Munich.

I was getting more and more disgusted with myself. All my life I had dreamed of a visit to the beautiful land in southern Germany. Now, while finally approaching it, I didn't feel anything at all. Something had gone wrong with me lately, and I couldn't figure it out. It was as if all feeling had left me.

Did Micherle notice my changed behaviour? I hardly noticed when she told me that she had met a young refugee and he had asked her to go along with him to Heidelberg. It didn't matter; nothing mattered any more. I nodded, and she left! Well, now I was alone! No more responsibility, no more need to talk to anybody.

There seemed to be no hope or help for me, and I was beyond the point of recognizing my need for help and trying to find it somewhere. Most likely nobody would have cared anyway. No doctors or nurses were available for all those thousands of refugees in every city. People either survived or went *kaputt*. When I had the opportunity years later, I told a doctor about those days and he said I had been at the verge of a nervous collapse.

A few days after my arrival in Munich I found myself early in the morning on a brooding street. My beclouded mind was wrestling; darkness seemed to press in from every side, and my head tried in vain to think. Past and present seemed to blend.

Was there still war? No, war had been over for five months. A strange silence covered the land. No more hammering of machine guns, no more explosions, no ominous droning of airplanes during the nights, no more screams and wild cries as bombs found their targets. It was unbelievably still, so oppressively calm.

But the big city carried the unconcealed wounds and marks of recent destruction. Ruins and fire-blackened trees edged the avenues, throwing long, strange shadows in the new morning light.

I wandered aimlessly through the streets. The stricken city tried to awaken. Bricks and rubbish had been pushed to the sides, making a path for the crowds. People rushed and pushed eagerly to get to shops and counters where they would stand in line for hours to buy a few morsels of food, if luck stayed by.

Working people made their way to their places of labour, streetcars overfilled with passengers clanged and banged impatiently. Bicyclists squeezed through throngs of pedestrians, frustrated and encumbered.

I stood and watched. There was no need for me to force my way; I had nowhere to go. With thousands of others I called "home" a little straw-covered square on the gym floor of an old half-destroyed school. And I was fortunate to have found that.

Having received my morning food, a bowl of thin soup and two pieces of dry bread, I was free to go and do as I pleased. Nobody cared if I didn't check in by nightfall, and many more new "numbers" waited for a vacant place on the straw as still more refugees flooded in from the East.

I watched the morning rush, studying passing faces— strange, emotionless faces, seemingly hard and unfeeling, without a smile. The memory of death and the present hunger were stamped on their sad eyes and bony cheeks. But it mattered little to me. I didn't expect a smile, not even a spoken word.

Looking up, surprised, I felt the sudden warmth of the sun through my thin, shabby jacket. Why was the sun shining? It had rained for so many weeks. Almost at every step of my westward flight, rain had drenched me mercilessly. Now the bright, cheery sun and those charred ruins around me didn't seem to fit together. I stood staring and wondering, trying to bring order into my muddled brain. My mind turned in senseless rotation the words *sun, rain, ruins, death, hunger.*

Oh, yes, I was hungry again! The two pieces of old bread did not last long enough, let alone the watery soup. Why, now, why did the sun shine?

A deep urge crept up my throat, an urge to cry, to let go, to feel again. But I could not do it; my smile and my tears seemed buried under an avalanche of horror. Oh, how much I wanted to feel those warm drops rolling down my cheeks. I tried and tried again, but I just couldn't cry. With a hopeless shrug of my shoulders I walked on.

Suddenly my eyes were caught by several printed announcements. Big letters notified the people that there would be a sacred concert that night. But where? At the far outskirts of the city stood a frail cathedral, cracked but still standing; the bombs must have missed it. Even the organ was still intact. A group of courageous string musicians were inviting everyone to an evening with Handel.

Music! Music? How long had it been since I had heard the sound of good music? It seemed so long ago, almost an eternity. Music belonged to a past world, a world I had no place or part in any more.

Would the people let me in? The sign said everybody was welcome. And what about money? I had none to spare. I had given everything of value to the guide who had led me across to the border. I had saved nothing but my life and the knapsack on my back.

I read the invitation again: "Free Entrance—No Admission Fee!"

This was unbelievable. Why would anything be free? Why would anyone make music for *me* voluntarily? I pondered the mystery. Yes, there would be a concert, real music, which I loved so much.

Suddenly I was part of the crowd. I pressed forward, elbowed my way into a streetcar, and asked with new self-confidence for the way to the cathedral. Surprisingly enough, people were willing to direct me without so much as a frown. I swallowed hard in astonishment.

For several hours I lingered around the cathedral until the people came and filed reverently, expectantly into the high, arched sanctuary. The air inside was heavy with incense.

Not daring to sit in a pew, I stood lonely and still with the late comers. The building eventually was filled. My eyes searched wonderingly about the church. Everything seemed unfamiliar and different. I looked up and down the curving lines of the Romanesque dome.

The entire inner ceiling was covered with an old painting. I recognized it as a reproduction of the famous Sistine Chapel ceiling, "The Creation of Adam" by Michelàngelo. God is reaching out to Adam. As his finger touches the finger of Adam, the spark of life enters the newly created form of the man, and he becomes a living soul.

Yes, I knew the picture, but I had forgotten the implication. As I gazed up, my mind struggled to get hold of something I had learned long ago at Mother's knee—something that had been part of my childhood. What was it that I tried to remember?

The music began. Strings and organ blended softly and harmoniously. The sound swelled, becoming louder and stronger, filling the old building, ascending to the dome, embracing the old cracked picture and finally bursting out through the broken, stained-glass windows with joyful ringing into the wide, star-filled night.

And then I remembered the story of the picture. Mother told it again, and I listened. Standing alone among the hundreds of quiet strangers I suddenly felt warmth within me. The ice in my innermost being broke. The music and Mother's words forced their way through the cracks of my broken soul. My eyes grew hot and moist, and my heart began to sing. Tears of joy rushed down my face, but not wanting to disturb the other listeners, I did not lift my hand to wipe my face. My heart cried out, "Mother, I can feel again; oh, Mother, where are you?"

When the music came to its glorious finale, I gazed up again. In the painting, God looked lovingly and longingly at Adam, and the man looked adoringly into God's eyes. But somehow they both seemed to look down at me, and I imagined I saw their eyes smiling.

Slowly I moved out, as the surging crowd caught me and

carried me through the large doorway in the back. Then I found myself under the dark, velvety sky and looked up again.

My mind was still searching and asking questions. There were so many things I could not understand, but it did not matter any more. My heart had tasted again one moment of peace. Maybe life could have a purpose after all, and maybe there was lasting peace somewhere, a peace I had known before and lost. Maybe I could go out and find it again. At least I could try!

I nodded a grateful good-bye to the dome of the cathedral, where the lights were going out one by one over the picture of God and Adam. I turned around, straightened up, and with new courage walked into the night through the ruins and rubbish. My heart sang, and it was a new song. Or was it an old, long-forgotten song?

# 13
## Starting Over

The world looked different when I woke up the next morning. The inner pressure had eased, and when I closed my eyes I could again see the picture and hear the beautiful music. As I wandered through the city, I found things I had not seen before. Autumn had come, and stepping over the majestic Alps, had begun to paint the land in bright and happy colours, even in the damaged city. The sun seemed to apologize for all the rain of the summer, for the Indian summer brought bright sunshine, deep blue skies, and fleecy white clouds. I had found a small park with benches, trees, and bushes left, and from there I watched the clouds, breathed in the pure air, and listened to the busy noises of a resurrecting city.

Other refugees had discovered those benches, too, and as we met over and over again, we began to nod shy greetings. Refugees are usually not the most sociable people, so I looked up surprised when one day a young man walked up beside me and introduced himself politely. Decent girls, I believed, did not make acquaintances with men in the streets. Street acquaintances were for cheap girls only. I raised my eyebrows in surprise and wondered what to do. Maybe it was the music still ringing in my heart, maybe the smiling blue sky or the white clouds that tumbled dreamily with the wind; but this time I smiled and answered with a few friendly words. He was a refugee also, from my homeland besides, and after a short time we had become friends. How nice!

Suddenly Gerhard, my new acquaintance, asked, "Miss Appelt, did you say you had educational training during the last years?"

"Yes," I nodded, "one could put it that way if necessary."

He got enthusiastic. "Do you know that you might be able to find a job? The state department of education and culture here in Munich is looking desperately for elementary-school teachers. Maybe you could apply."

I shook my head. "No, sir, I have no chance. They will not hire Nazi leaders, and I had a high rank in the Hitler Youth. They would catch up with me sooner or later; besides, I would not want to lie!"

'But you don't understand, *Fräulein*. They give amnesty to Hitler Youth members. As long as you were not a party member you will be OK."

Suddenly I was interested. No, I had not been a party member, only a member of the Hitler Youth movement. Somehow life had been so busy that our school had never found the time to stage the important ceremony of enrolling us in the party.

"But I have no papers with me to prove my education or anything. How would anybody hire me for any job?"

"Never mind, *Fräulein*. Try it anyway and see. You don't need to tell them everything anyhow! The new Bavarian government is determined to reopen at least the elementary schools at the end of October, and there is a great lack of teachers. Nazi members cannot be rehired, by order of the military government. You have nothing to lose, young lady; try it'!'

He was right—I had nothing to lose. But how would I go about it?

He seemed to read my thoughts. "I will be glad to help you find the right office," he volunteered. "How about tomorrow morning?"

I smiled at his eagerness. Why was he so interested in helping me? It must be the same incomprehensible motive that had compelled the American soldiers to help us, the Red Cross lady from Switzerland to organize refugee stations, the string musicians to make music for us—free. I couldn't understand it, but I had begun to accept it as something real and true even though I had no name for it.

Hitler had taught me many things: pride, perseverance, logic, morals, efficiency. But I did not consciously know what love was, kind neighbourly love that cares without being forced to do so. My experiences with Russian soldiers after the war had erased the remnants of my faith in humanity, and I could only wonder when someone showed me kindness.

"Yes," I heard myself saying, "I will meet you here tomorrow morning at nine o'clock. And thank you so much for your kindness."

The young man shook my hand, and we parted, smiling.

I found a way to iron my best dress, stood in a long line to wait my turn for a shower, and got my hair done in a beauty parlour after endless hours of waiting, for there was no hot water to get it washed otherwise.

Arriving at our meeting place the next morning, I found the tall young *Landsmann* (man of my homeland) already waiting. He looked surprised and eyed me from head to toe.

"Do I look all right for that interview?" I felt uneasy under his searching gaze.

"Oh, yes," he said, blushing a little. "I think you look very nice." Then it was my turn to feel flushed with embarrassment. We began to walk toward the centre of the city.

He asked if he could meet me the next day to see how I

fared. Then he gave me more advice on what to say, and left. I walked up some broad steps into a building.

I felt scared and lonely. In my hand I clutched a paper, the only document I possessed—my Catholic baptismal certificate. All I was able to prove was that I had been born, baptized, and named after my poor mother.

Presently I found myself seated across a desk from an elderly gentleman, who asked in a friendly Bavarian drawl, "What do you want, my girl?"

I had planned my speech and reviewed it in my mind as I tried to sleep on the straw-covered gym floor—but suddenly I couldn't say it! No, here again was someone kind, friendly, and human. Why should I try to deceive him?

I simply told the truth. I described my training, my bitter disappointment when I learned that the Nazis had lied, my lack of papers to prove anything. But I assured him I had a great desire to learn all over and be of service if given a chance.

I lifted my tear-filled eyes up and—was it possible? The man wasn't by any chance wiping his eyes! Why should he?

"Little girl," he said, "would you be willing to take a special examination before we make any further plans?"

"Oh, yes, I will be glad to!" I nodded eagerly, drying my eyes.

The man did some telephoning, and I was sent to different rooms for testing. In the afternoon I returned to the first office and the friendly old man received me with a smile.

"You did very well on your examinations," he said pleasantly. "Now for the other parts. We can give you an emergency certificate, and you will be included in a further training programme while you teach, to prepare you for your final state examination. There is just one question left: What religion do you claim?"

I hesitated, not knowing what to say. Did I have any religion?

The man continued: "You see, southern Bavaria is Catholic all the way through and the people resent teachers of other convictions."

"But, sir, I am a Catholic," I interrupted, and fumbled for my birth certificate.

"Can you prove it?"

I handed him the certificate. He studied it carefully, compared my application blanks and the document, stood up, and offered me his hand. "You are hired!"

I received further orders, a train ticket, and a letter of recommendation. I would leave the next day.

I must be dreaming again! No longer an unwanted refugee, I was a normal, respectable person again. I had become a teacher, hired by the democratic Bavarian government to teach the primary grades in Grossding-harding in the southern part of Bavaria. How could so many good things happen at once?

I met Gerhard the next morning to thank him and to tell him good-bye. He seemed sober and had a lonely look in his grey eyes, a look we refugees had learned to recognize as a part of our lives. I beamed and bubbled as I told him of my good fortune. We shook hands and parted. He looked sad. Weeks later it dawned on me that my leaving might have destroyed a small flame of hope in his heart. He seemed to be such a pleasant person! Our paths never crossed again.

The Alps thrust their snow-covered peaks into a gilded sky at the far southern end of the high plateau, which my train slowly crossed. My new school could not be reached directly by train; I had to walk several miles from the station. My principal received me in a very friendly manner after he had read the letter of introduction I handed him. He invited me to stay at his house until I found permanent lodging.

One unforgettable incident took place while I was a guest there. The principal's wife had served a simple supper, and I was invited. After the meal she took a large, red, yellow-streaked apple from the cupboard and handed it to me. Overwhelmed by this gesture, I broke into tears. The lady looked perplexed.

"Ma'am," I stammered, "I think I have forgotten how an apple tastes. Would you permit me to save this apple for a few days so I could enjoy the smell?"

"You eat it," she said, "and I will give you another one when you leave!"

I could hardly get myself to eat that apple, that wine-red, luscious, aromatic piece of wonder. I had not seen, smelled, or eaten an apple since I left the hospital the year before, and I ate it with reverence. She forgot to give the second apple when I left her home—she had her cupboard full of apples—and my disappointment was so great that I had to fight back my tears.

Teaching was fun! It took a while to understand the Bavarian dialect of those little farmer children, but we enjoyed each other from the very first day. What a way of teaching it was, though! Even chalk had to be used with care, otherwise I would run out before the next ration came in. But we made satisfactory progress, and the parents seemed pleased.

One first-grade boy, above the others, seemed to love me with all his little heart. His parents had a small homestead near the school. He was the baby, born after the other children had grown up and left. Whenever I stepped out of the school building where I had my own cramped room upstairs, I would find him sitting on the front step waiting for me. I had made it a custom to go for a long walk every afternoon. After the rainy summer, the autumn was unusually sunny and clear, and into November and December the days remained bright and pleasant. I never seemed to get enough of the beautiful view of the Alps, which I could see from my classroom window. My daily walks became my homage to that breathtaking scenery. My young friend, Sepperl, walked with me, his soft hand slipped quietly in mine. He would talk or be silent, as he chose. It was obvious that his innocent little heart worshiped his first-grade teacher, and my heart was warmed by his evident affection.

One day, as I checked the homework, Sepperl had not done his assignment. "Sepperl," I said firmly, "if you don't do your homework you cannot go with teacher for walks any more!"

His big blue eyes stared at me with a hurt expression. Slowly big tears covered the deep blue star-like eyes and rolled down the soft, round cheeks. I quickly turned away.

"You've got to be firm, Maria," I told myself, "or Sepperl will think he can get away with things because he is your little companion."

But those big, tear-filled blue eyes haunted me. After school I hurried to go for my walk so I could soften the blow for Sepperl. But Sepperl was not sitting on the steps as he usually did. "Well, maybe he is making up his homework," I mumbled, and went alone. The next morning Sepperl was not at school. Perhaps, like some of the others, he had come down with the flu. Poor little fellow! I cut out some pictures for him during recess. I would go and take them to him in the evening.

When I came back from my walk, a messenger waited. Would I go right away to see Sepperl, please? He was critically ill.

I flew up the stairs to my room for the pictures, and then to Sepperl's house. As I entered the small, dark home, I heard the wailing of Sepperl's mother. My heart skipped a beat! Why was she wailing so loud? Didn't she know better? Sepperl needed quietness and rest! I raced upstairs to his chamber and froze in horror. Candles had been lighted, and the mother and father knelt by his bed. Sepperl was dead.

Heartbroken I threw myself over the limp little figure and cried, "Sepperl, wake up!"

But his face felt cold, and his eyes were closed. His little white hands were folded neatly and didn't move.

The parents led me downstairs and told me the story. They had thought he had a cold and had put him to bed. When the mother came back after a while to see how he was doing, he seemed to be choking. They sent for the doctor in the next town immediately. When after a few hours he arrived, he diagnosed it as diphtheria and could give little hope. The child suffocated. "He called for you, teacher," the mother sobbed, "but you were gone!"

I do not know how I managed to teach the next few days. At the funeral I sat with the relatives by request of the parents and sobbed so heart-brokenly that the mother tried to comfort me. Yes, she was a good Catholic and she believed that the boy had gone to heaven. But I had no hope. True, I attended the Catholic mass because it was the thing to do in that community, but I didn't believe in life after death or any other religious doctrine. All I could see was the withdrawn, grave, waxen face in a small, white casket. And when I closed my eyes, I could see his two big, blue eyes as they had slowly filled with tears. Why? O fate, why?

I lingered at his grave, not knowing what to do with myself. Suddenly I felt a strong hand taking mine and a friendly voice said softly, "*Schulfräulein,* your grief will not bring him back. Don't cry any more, please!"

Looking up, I saw two sincere blue eyes, a mass of curly blond hair, and white teeth in a big, boyish smile. I recognized him as one of the young farmers of the area to whom I had been introduced some weeks before at a wedding dance. We left the graveyard together and walked along the same path I had enjoyed so often with my little pupil. As the evening shadows lengthened, I began to tell him about that incident in class. Franzl listened patiently, then spoke. He spoke without polish, with plain words, but his simple explanations comforted me more than any deep philosophy. My guilt and sorrow began to lift, and when at last I climbed the stairs to my room, I felt able to face life again.

He and I became fast friends. The community began to whisper as we appeared everywhere together. I felt a little worried about the whole thing. One of his friends told me that Franzl's parents gave him a hard time. He was the heir to one of the richest farms in the county, and I was poor as a mouse in comparison.

At Christmas he brought me a piece of heirloom jewellery intended to be worn by the future wife of that family's heir. My head spun! His mother had sent the gift to me. The son had won the family over, but did I want that?

Two weeks after Christmas I received an emergency visit from my supervisor. He urgently needed a new teacher for a village school twenty kilometres to the south. It would be no easy task. Since the government had put a refugee camp into the former dance hall of that village, the number of students had grown too great for the school's single classroom, and I would have to teach in two shifts. No books, no teaching help, eight grades, the responsibilities of a principal on top of the long teaching hours, dealing with the community and a stubborn school board—the job was enough to scare anyone. That's why the supervisor hadn't found a teacher for that place.

"Are you aware of my age, sir?" I asked.

"Yes, Miss Appelt." He bowed politely. "But I think you can do it."

"I will try, if you will back me up," I promised.

I packed my few belongings, visited a little snow-covered

grave once more, and left a friendly community behind me—and a very unhappy young man.

Would my heart ever find a home again? I did not feel that I had been cut out to be a Bavarian farmer's wife. That old German saying sounded convincing that Alpine flowers do not thrive well in other soil; and strange flowers, on the other hand, tend to wilt in the Alps. I knew I competed as a strange flower among the native girls, and they had let me know about it!

Why had I accepted so hard a job? Maybe it had been a welcome escape. Maybe it was my nature. Certainly I had a challenge on my hands. I busied myself in my many new tasks from the day of my arrival. The presiding *Bürgermeister* of the village acted understandingly and friendly and helped me get started.

# 14
## Whirlwind

After a few days in my new post an intriguing idea struck me. The neighbouring village had not been able to reopen its school for lack of a teacher, and suddenly I thought of Annemarie, Rudy's sister, in northern Bavaria. We had exchanged letters after postal service had begun, and I knew she looked for a job. I told my supervisor about her. He reacted with enthusiasm in spite of the fact that she belonged to the Lutheran Church, and I invited her to come and visit me.

They hired her at once, and from the beginning we immensely enjoyed working together. We planned, tried new methods, helped each other in many problems, and roomed together in my school apartment. The pupils made good progress, and the parents began to accept us as their friends. They customarily invited the two *Schulfräuleins* to weddings, dances, and church feasts. Soon we had a reputation as good dancers and our lives filled to the brim with social events. Life had turned almost normal for us, even pleasant, except for shortages of material things, but that was not important to people brought back from death.

Into this calm scene descended a bomb—or was it a whirlwind? There had been a school holiday, and I had gone back to my former school community to visit friends. There my blond farmer friend insisted that I spend some time in his house. Knowing the custom of the land, I realized he was trying to compel me to make a decision. A boy didn't bring a girl home to his parents unless he had honest intentions of marriage. I felt uneasy, but yielded to his urging and visited his parents.

While we made small talk, the telephone rang. Franzl answered and looked surprised. "It's for you, Maria Anne!"

"For me? Who would call me? Nobody knows I am at your house but Annemarie."

It was Annemarie. She had found a telephone in the mayor's office. She sounded choked and excited. "Maria Anne," she stuttered, "I just got a letter from my mother. The International Red Cross has found my brother! He is alive and on his way to see my parents. I know he will come down to see us. What shall I answer my mother?"

What should I say? Franzl stood beside me, waiting and wondering. My own heart and head spun like a wild carousel. And Annemarie, at the other end of the line cried and laughed at the same time. I knew what it meant to her; she had worshipped her brother.

Well, I had to answer. "Tell your brother that he is more than welcome to visit you, Annemarie! After all, dear, he is the brother of my best friend, and I will accept him as such. Annemarie I am so happy that he is alive. I know what it means to you and your family. You know my personal attitude; as long as he respects it, everything will be all right."

I had to be alone and collect my thoughts. I excused myself as soon as possible and in deepest turmoil returned home immediately. The past was coming alive again, and fear gripped me. But Annemarie bubbled over with joy. She had already sent a letter telling Rudy to come and had made a thousand plans.

He came! It was April, and a late snow had covered the land.

Late in the evening, just as we were ready to retire, I answered a knock on the door and saw two men in navy-blue suits. Rudy stood before me, slim and haggard, while his friend, Riko, seemed to poke him from behind. Both looked cold and hungry.

"Welcome, and come in," I said with forced cheerfulness, and shook hands with both.

Our hearth beamed warmth, and we soon had hot food ready for the weary travellers. Rudy didn't say much, but sat quietly trying to warm his cold, wet feet. Annemarie busied herself getting places ready for the boys to sleep, and I tried to keep conversation going. I couldn't help feeling sorry for Rudy. He had changed so much. All his youthful assurance was gone, and he seemed depressed and lonely. I knew how he felt. His whole world had broken, just as mine had; only he had not yet managed to pick up the leftover pieces.

The tension eased after a few days, and Rudy and I slowly found a way to talk. I watched myself carefully so that my heart would not slip again, because I was more determined than ever not to fall in love with him again. Rudy had just the opposite idea, as I found out later.

He applied at the University of Munich to study philosophy and was accepted. Munich was only a few hours away from my school and Rudy had every reason to return to my place every so often since his sister lived with me. He had never been a man of many words but he worked his way into my heart again by his quiet determination and his gentle disposition.

The breaking up with my jolly farmer friend left me overly sensitive and I felt guilty and resentful, but Rudy's patience and his arguments won out. I had no choice—Rudy needed me! He loved me, I was finally convinced of that, and I had loved him for too long to be unreasonable, but what he couldn't understand was that I wasn't the same girl he had proposed to just two years earlier. The thought of marriage frightened me. I didn't feel ready for it and I wondered if I ever would.

When Rudy had put his ring on my finger that unforgettable summer before the war ended, I had been a young, sheltered girl, full of romantic dreams and plans. Now I felt weary and disillusioned about love and life and I dreaded many things.

I dreaded the physical relationship of marriage. Would I be able to shake the memories of drunken soldiers grabbing for girls? Would I be able to forget Helga's white face pleading for help? But I hid my fears and smiled and we announced our engagement and the wedding date. Rudy was radiant, almost like his old, confident self again. He didn't seem to notice how quiet and thin I was getting—my ulcers acted up again, and it wasn't just my fear of marriage that started it either.

Our engagement had caused unexpected trouble in other ways, too. Of all things, we experienced difficulties because of religion. It was a cruel joke, for neither of us had any belief of any kind, but I was a Catholic by baptism and by convenience since my job demanded it. I had never had any Catholic upbringing, but now I attended the Catholic Church every Sunday. Carefully I had watched every movement of other churchgoers, learning the form of worship and thus fitting myself into the community customs. Other than that I didn't even bother to give religion any consideration. Neither did Rudy. He was a a Protestant, nominal only, but foolish enough to tell that to my priest. That was the beginning of "cold war" between the two! I stood in the middle.

The priest of the area, a feared and highly respected figure, had never been my friend. I avoided him. When I announced my engagement, he felt it his duty to stop our marriage. As was the custom, I had to attend a preparatory catechism for marriage. Since Rudy was not a Catholic, he did not attend these lectures and I went alone.

How I dreaded every lecture. The priest reminded me of my foster father—so full of zeal, but with no love! He threatened with hell fire and condemnation if I didn't give Rudy up. I looked up, tortured, and pleaded:

"Reverend Father, please try to understand! My fiancé needs me. I cannot let him go, for his sake. He lost everything —his home, his career, his future. He might go the wrong way if I turn my back on him. Can't you understand? He is a human being—there is a human responsibility!"

But the man in the black robe shook his head. No, he couldn't understand and he threatened not to perform the marriage. That would have been a catastrophe, because a ceremony before the judge alone would not have been accepted as legal by the community. I *had* to get married in the church.

Rudy was no help. He still had some rough Navy manners that irritated me to no end. He insulted the priest, teased me about my sensitivity, and caused tensions in the community.

A very influential farmer whose many children I taught and adored stepped in at last and helped us out. He talked to his friend the bishop and we received permission to be married. Rudy was triumphant. Now the priest had to marry us.

Our wedding became a community affair. Pupils and parents showered us with gifts and attention. All my small pupils strewed flowers and lined the aisles with lighted candles as we entered the nine-hundred-year-old church, filled to the walls with people and flowers, the smell of incense heavy in the air. With a face of stone the priest united us. Rudy felt too happy to be mean and was more than willing to bury the battle axe, but the priest was not.

After an elaborate dinner, my husband and I danced the wedding dance according to an old Bavarian custom, while the other people formed a large circle and watched. When we finished our waltz, the rest of the dancers joined us. Long after we had left the dance floor, we could still hear the music of the brass band and the stomping of many feet, clear into the early morning. Yes, it had been a gala occasion for everybody. Villagers talked about the *Schulfräulein's* wedding for a long time —longer than we did!

We had no honeymoon; Rudy had to return to the university after the weekend, and I continued teaching. He did not like to leave me every Monday morning, because my health began to fail again. I became frightfully thin and pale and began to fear the darkness. The priest felt it his religious duty to threaten me every so often that our marriage would not last, and life seemed to get more and more difficult. Rudy and I had a hard time adjusting to our new way of life. We both tried hard, but slipped deeper into misunderstandings and estrangement. We were not the same young people who had wandered so happily among the flowering meadows just two years before.

After our first year of marriage, which was a nightmare, I was convinced I had made a mistake in marrying Rudy. Maybe I had no potential as a good wife. Maybe we were just incompatible. I thought I had found a new beginning, but it seemed only the beginning of a bitter end. Rudy and I were ready to give up.

# 15
# The Old Book

In our little living room, just below the ceiling in the corner, hung a small crucifix. A Catholic farmer's wife had brought it to me as a gift before I got married.

"You can't start a marriage without him in your home," she had said, very motherly and very pious. She had told me to pray the Lord's Prayer and some Hail Mary's before the cross five times every day. Obediently I had hung the crucifix where she had suggested. I tried to be obliging and avoid hurt feelings, but I had never been able to say the prayers; it would have been hypocrisy. It was bad enough that I had to act religious in church, but I would never pray to that Jesus in my home. The Nazis had taught me he was an imposter, the illegitimate child of a Jewish girl by a Roman soldier. I would have nothing to do with such a person.

It had been another rough weekend between Rudy and me, and he had left for a week of studies at the University in Munich, where he had switched to studying law. I knew that my husband was desperate; he wanted to save our marriage. But I was too worn out to care any more. I felt glad that he had gone for another week. Everything seemed so hopeless. We lived in two different worlds and couldn't fit together. Our ethical principles clashed constantly. My past made marriage unbearable for me. I couldn't forget the brutality I had seen, and estrangement held me at the same time Rudy did. How far apart can two people be while sleeping in the same bed?

Not until our marriage did I realize how great our differences were. I had little knowledge of the life Rudy had led up to the day of our wedding. It had been unusual, to say the least! After a short time in a prisoner-of-war camp he had established himself on the black market as a cigarette trader. His knowledge of the English language helped. He bought cigarettes from the Allied soldiers for one German mark apiece and sold them to nicotine-hungry German customers for five to seven marks. His business had flourished and he was known in certain circles as the "cigarette king". At times he had thousands of cigarettes stored in his apartment. Never in his life had Rudy done manual labour; it was beneath him.

I hated this illegal business and insisted that a hard day's work never degraded anybody. But what would happen to Rudy if I divorced him? I had seen a lawyer already and he wondered if there might be a chance to annul our marriage. That sounded good to me. But what about Rudy? Would it leave him scarred for life? His love for me seemed to deepen in proportion to our insoluble difficulties; he was not ready to let me go.

I looked up at the cross: "You surely haven't done much for this home, Christ," I said defiantly. On a sudden impulse I stepped on a chair and took the cross down and put it in the closet. I didn't care any more what my motherly farmer friend would say. But the empty spot on the wall seemed to bother me more than the cross, and my mind would go back to that naked, bruised figure in the closet.

Five Lord's Prayers, the woman had said. Did I know the Lord's Prayer by heart? Sure, I joined in every Sunday in church when the people chanted and I murmured with the students when we had morning prayer.

"Our Father," I thought. Well, I could acknowledge a God if I had to. That was feasible since Hitler had taught us to believe in a supreme power, as long as it wasn't that Jesus Christ. But "Father"? Never mind! Who needed a father, anyway? Someone who looked down on me, scolding, punishing, demanding—I could never please him even if I tried. But that wasn't my greatest concern. It was that man on the cross. Sure, my mother believed in him, but was he really there when she needed him? "God, where is Mother? I have nightmares and I dream every so often—I see her homeless, wandering from place to place, hungry, alone, lost, like the many old refugee women I passed on the way to the West. Mother is dying of hunger in my dreams. You, God, are you looking after her? I don't ask anything for me, but care for *her* if you are up there, God; don't let her suffer!"

I had said it aloud and my voice startled me in the stillness of my lonely apartment. What was wrong with me? Was I by any chance praying? Well, if it did Mother any good, I could say *ten* Lord's Prayers a day! I would burn a hundred candles, too. And I would do the same for Rudy.

Mother and Rudy, the two people I worried most about— I would do anything to see them happy. But religion was a fairy tale to me—and life was not!

My classroom had been my refuge and a haven of peace. My pupils and I understood each other. We loved each other, harmonized with each other. The more conflicts I faced the more I fled to my teaching for relief. But lately I wasn't even finding peace in the classroom.

Whenever I looked up from my desk I looked at a cross. By rules of the church, every school in our area had a large cross on the wall. The pupils would turn to it when praying.

I couldn't remember much about the cross-story any more,

just that the Jews had shouted, "His blood may come upon us and our children". I remembered what the SS teacher had said —the Jews were cursed for killing him—but why? Why couldn't I remember more about those things? The haziness in my head increased again and I felt trapped—caged like an animal by friction, pressures, and agony. Wouldn't it have been better if I had died during the war like my friend Fluntl? At least he had died feeling victorious—died for a cause—now there was nothing left to live or die for. Miserable existence!

Rudy walked in Friday night with a big smile. He had a new bounce in his step. What was he up to now? I put up all my defences. No new upsets for me, please. My stomach already felt as if it had a hundred knives in it.

"Look what I have!" Rudy looked sheepish and a bit embarrassed. He unwrapped an old, black book and handed it to me.

"A Bible?" I felt blank and puzzled. "What are you doing with a Bible, man? And where did you find it?" I bit my tongue and swallowed the rest of my words, for I almost asked, "Did you steal it?"

Rudy had no qualms about taking certain things if he needed or wanted them. It was in the spirit of a lost war to help yourself to anything you could, except that I couldn't, and Rudy and I had big arguments about it.

Rudy seemed to know what I thought, and he hastened to explain. "I found it in a used book store—very cheap!"

"Why did you get it?"

Rudy hesitated for a moment. "I fell into conversation with a young fellow on my way to the railway last Monday morning. He is only a kid, really, but he knows religion. He reads his Bible so much he knows it all by heart. He belongs to one of those sects and sounds a bit mixed up, but he says the Catholics are wrong and he can prove it from the Bible so I decided to start reading it to tell that priest off!"

I nodded. That sounded like Rudy, all right. He would go

to any length to get even with the priest—even to the absurd extreme of reading the Bible. And he did! Every time I turned around he sat with that old book, and seemed very engrossed. That was fine with me because we had a smoother weekend. But not all smooth, of course—we had one big fight about the priest.

I wanted Rudy to let matters go and attend church with me. After all, my teaching job provided for both of us and his university studies, and I needed good relations with the priest to keep my job. But Rudy couldn't see it. So I walked to church alone and Rudy stayed at home reading his old Bible.

As I watched the priest performing his rituals, I wondered. That man did what he felt was right. He was true to his convictions, and I had always begrudgingly respected him for it. But Rudy had convictions too! So did I. Was there no way to bring people together if they had differences of opinions? Why was religion a divider?

Not until a few weeks later did Rudy dare to tell me the whole truth about his new interest. He hadn't only started to read the Bible; he had also visited a Protestant preacher in his eagerness to prove the priest wrong.

"I asked the man to give me some hard facts against the Catholic Church," Rudy said, and I nodded. That was my husband, all right.

"Did he?" I asked, and felt scared.

"No." Rudy sounded perplexed. "That fellow said he couldn't do that. His religion was something too precious to be used to fight anyone with."

"Good." I felt relieved, but not for long.

"Well, I think I found a way to get my needed information yet. I joined a Bible study group in the city!"

"You are joking. *You*, with such people?" I didn't know if I should laugh or cry.

"Schatzi (little treasure), it's interesting, really! Did you know that the Bible is deeply entwined with ancient history?"

Knowing Rudy's love for history, I now understood his enthusiasm.

"I don't remember much about the Bible any more, though I grew up with it," I said, deep in thought. "But you know how I feel about any history right now."

How did I feel? Bitter! I hated history and disliked teaching it. History had been one of my favourite subjects in Nazi training but now I detested it. History writers were manipulators, liars who tried to show their own side of the story, not true facts. Hitler had used history to prove that his Third Reich would stand a thousand years, but it had crumbled in twelve years. Fooey on history!

"Schatzi," Rudy said very gently, "those Christian people I meet with every week have something. I don't know what it is, but it's something special. They might help me to become a better person, and I want to change, Maria Anne. I want to in order to save our marriage!"

I was touched. I never had thought that Rudy would go to such lengths to keep me, but it was hard to picture Rudy as a religious person.

"I mean," Rudy said as an afterthought, "I don't intend to join any church, but I'll get enough Christianity to make me a better person. Then I'll stop. I don't want to become totally involved, of course. After all, that would be intellectual suicide."

"Rudy," I said, "maybe I should study some, too. After all, I could use some changing for the better and learn to hold my temper. Maybe you could teach me what you are learning every week?"

But Rudy had a better idea. He found an old, retired minister who was willing to visit us every weekend who would introduce both of us to religion and doctrines.

Precious old Brother Schneider! Will he ever know until we meet in eternity what he did for us!

It wasn't so much what he said, though he knew his Bible well, admonished us with conviction, and was very fundamental and convincing—it was his life that impressed us the most.

It was winter when he began his visits, Bavarian winter. We lived at the foot of the Alps and one night could bury us in snow up to the eaves. His shoes were leaky, his coat old and threadbare, but snowstorm or sunshine, ice or slush, that old man came walking miles from the railway station to my schoolhouse, having a cheery "*Guten abend*" and no complaints though his hands were often stiff and his lips blue from the cold.

He brought me my own Bible, a translation by Martin Luther.

"What is it that makes the old man come out in the worst weather?" Rudy asked repeatedly after the minister had left us to visit other people in the mountains. "What is in the deal for him? It couldn't be just his great concern for my rotten soul. Or *is* he really that worried about our spiritual welfare?"

He was, and we knew it, though he was a strict man who had strange manners. He assigned us a passage to read in the Bible every week, and we read it to show our appreciation for his willingness to come.

He came until Rudy asked him not to return. Brother Schneider didn't ask why; he just said a kind "Good-bye," said a prayer and left with a smile.

I knew why Rudy wanted to stop studying religion; it was getting under his skin. Brother Schneider was a godly man, but he believed tolerance to be of the devil. He talked just like the priest in one respect: in order to accept God, he taught, a person had to choose sides. And both preachers felt they were on the right side! Because Brother Schneider wasn't Catholic, he felt sure they were on the wrong side. That was one thing Rudy appreciated and fully agreed with. But he was not so much against the priest that he wanted to join another faith. As a matter of fact, Rudy's antagonism against the priest had almost vanished as he had got so interested in Christ's teachings. But join a Protestant or any other church? He could never go that far!

How long, however, can ice withstand warmth? Can winter hold the earth in bondage when the spring sun kisses the soil alive to flowers and fruit?

Rudy and I had left ourselves open too long to the warmth of the gospel story, and we could not close our minds to it any more if we had to. We could not leave our Bibles alone long enough to forget their message, and I didn't want to. For that matter, neither did Rudy!

We both admitted by then that the Bible *is* God's Word, and the agreement became the common denominator for our different personalities. We both realized that it was God who had brought us safely through the war, spared our lives, and brought us together in marriage. It was only fair and the right thing to do to serve him in return.

While we struggled for a final decision, God sent us some extra help—I found out that Mother was alive! The International Red Cross located her in West Germany in a refugee camp. Through her letters I found out that her husband had died and that all of her children except the oldest son, August, who had stayed in Czechoslovakia with his Czech wife, were safe in the West. We all had homes and each wanted to keep her, but Mother went to live with her second oldest daughter because she was sick and needed Mother most.

I longed so much to see her but I had to wait for long, long months. Travelling was so difficult and costly those days; it was next to impossible to get a travel permit without bribing and we were poor. Her letters made the waiting bearable and what she wrote warmed our hearts. God was so real to her— and so good. He had made all of his promises come true in her life while she had gone through the ordeals of banishment from her little home. In his grace he had laid the father, ill with cancer, to rest before the Czech order of expulsion came. Mother's letters reflected so much hope, serenity, and joy in the Lord that we couldn't help but covet her peace of mind. We wanted what she had.

By early summer we chose the side that seemed right for us and were baptized into church membership. We also took the consequences: it was only a matter of time (but more time than I ever expected) before I was without a job. Protestant teachers don't teach in Catholic communities in southern Bavaria. I knew that; I understood and respected it, and I left—but I had no place to go!

Somehow I had the idea that God would do something special for us because we had decided to serve him. I thought he would baby me and keep all hardship away because I didn't feel capable of facing a storm.

But God knew what was needed—and the storm came. I was bent over with the pain of my ulcerated stomach, undernourished and nervous, depressed and in tears most of the time. When the doctor confirmed my suspicion that I was pregnant, my heart sank. I felt completely unprepared to become a mother!

In the spring we moved into an attic room of an old farmhouse. A brick chimney that stood in the middle of the room spread heat three times a day, whenever the farmer downstairs made a fire. This was a blessing while the weather was cool, but not when summer came.

Rudy stopped his studies at the University of Munich. Knowing he had to support a wife and soon a baby also, he went out looking for a job. I stayed in our little room, praying and waiting.

What lonely days! It would have been wiser for us to leave the community, but we couldn't because the housing authorities would not transfer us. Besides, it would have taken a lot of money to bribe a landlord in the city to rent us a place to stay.

Every evening Rudy came home weary and discouraged. He could not find a job with so many odds against him. He was a refugee with a Prussian accent, and refugees were not in demand especially *Saupreussen* (Bavarian slang for Germans from the north). Besides, as a former Nazi officer, he was watched very closely by the American military government. No former Nazi must be allowed to make a comeback in the civil service. Rudy had no references, or, for that matter, experience in any trade. His identification card classified him as a university student, and employers shied away from training students for a trade. Students didn't usually stay long enough to make the training worthwhile, but returned to school as soon as possible.

The odds were against us and we knew it. Rudy could not find any job whatsoever—not even ditch-digging or street-sweeping.

After several weeks Rudy began to get desperate. I had tried to keep a smile on my face; but the new life within me was growing, and I anxiously counted the weeks until our baby's birth.

We lived as frugally as possible, but our few marks' savings melted away like snow in the spring sun. One morning we had to sit down and face facts. We counted our money. We had six marks (60p) left. Besides our own money, we had some paper notes in an old envelope. It wasn't much, but it seemed like a large sum because we had almost nothing else. It was our tithe. We had saved it up for many months. We had not turned it in to our church treasury, mainly because we seldom attended church in the city.

That morning I brought the envelope out, after we had counted our own last few marks, and laid it beside the money box. Somehow, managing to hold my tears back, I said:

"Remember what Brother Schneider told us about the tithe? It is God's money, and we must never touch it, not even when in need. He said the truth and we know it. Now, Rudy, the moment our money is gone we shall be tempted to touch what belongs to God, so we must not keep it under our roof any longer. You must take the morning train to the city, find the church treasurer, and give her the money." Rudy nodded, and his sad eyes revealed what he thought. Before he left we knelt together in prayer, and this was the gist of it:

"Lord, we have come to the end of our road. We have given up everything we had for our new belief, and it seems that you have forsaken us. If we have done wrong and this is our punishment, please show us why we are punished, because we don't know why! God, maybe we have believed a lie, made up by men. Maybe there is no God and nobody hears us as we pray. But if you are, O God, reveal yourself soon, for we cannot go on much longer. Everyone laughs at us already, and our own relatives think we have gone crazy. O Lord, if you are, bring help soon and listen to our pleading, for we ask in the name of your Son, Jesus, in whom we now believe. Amen."

We rose from our knees with heavy hearts, but I smiled and waved to Rudy as he walked away. Then, as soon as he was gone I threw myself on my bed and sobbed. Maybe Rudy's father was right. Maybe it was all my fault. Rudy had accepted our new religion first of all because he loved me and wanted to save our marriage. Sure, he believed in God, but somehow his whole religious experience was tied to his love for me. I felt a great responsibility, since Rudy expected me to lead out in spiritual matters. Alas! Somewhere I had made a mistake, for I had led Rudy and our marriage to a dead-end road, or so it seemed. My heart cried to God, and my tears mingled with my prayers. Doubts and darkness pressed in on me like a fog. Six more weeks before the baby was due, and nothing was ready— nothing was left for us. O God, why?

When Rudy returned, I tried to be brave and calm for his sake, and even managed a smile when he stepped in.

To my amazement, Rudy's face was one big smile. "What happened, dear?" I asked, hardly daring to believe my eyes.

"*Liebling* (darling), I found a job today." Rudy took me in his arms.

Fighting the bothersome tears back, I begged for details.

Rudy said he had battled with temptation and discouragement as he walked the long kilometre to the railway station and travelled to the city. He had prayed earnestly and had gone straight to the church office to find the lady who managed the church finances. He was afraid to keep our tithe money in his pocket while searching for work again.

The lady, surprised and pleased when Rudy handed her the money, asked the usual questions about our well-being. Rudy told her about our coming baby and his need for a job.

"Wait a few moments." The kind woman picked up the telephone and made several calls. Then she turned to Rudy. "Brother Hirschmann, I think we have found a job for you. Go to this address right away and ask for Mr. Bauer."

She wrote an address on a piece of paper and handed it to Rudy. He was too surprised to say much, but managed to thank the dear woman warmly before he hurried away.

Mr. Bauer interviewed Rudy briefly and hired him.

"Think of it, dear," Rudy reflected. "For so many weeks I have looked everywhere to find work, but not until we had turned in our tithe was God able to help us. It took only half an hour after I had turned in our tithe to find that job. Now I know God lives and cares!"

We prayed a different prayer that night, a prayer of thanksgiving and praise. Not even the oppressive heat of our attic room bothered us, so happy were we. We sat at the open window and watched the glimmering stars while our hearts conversed with God.

"God," I pleaded humbly, "forgive my doubts; for now I know that you are; and not only that, but God, you are love."

I thought the stars smiled as they twinkled. They reminded me of the time when Rudy and I had first met, and we had sat on that log to watch our friends the stars. Then love had begun to bind our hearts together, and now love was again weaving. But this time it was greater love, for God was in it.

# 16
# The Awesome Jew

Things improved slowly but steadily for us after that evening when Rudy came home to tell me about his new job. Sure, we had rough going for quite a while, but Rudy was so willing to do almost anything, and I was used to pinching pennies. Rudy's was a humble, low-paid job, and for the first time in his life the only son of the rich Hirschmann house did manual labour. He had to wrap packages from morning to evening and then deliver the packages to the railway terminal. The factory in which he worked manufactured sport and ski clothing. The company owner had once been a European ski champion, whose name, plus the quality of his merchandise, helped the company grow. The number of packages increased, and Rudy often had to work overtime.

In due time our baby arrived. We named her Christel. The cutest girl who ever arrived on this globe—naturally—she was so tiny that people seemed to see only her long dark hair, big brown eyes, and long dark eyelashes. We had named her after Rudy's mother, and the grandparents were so delighted about her that they could talk of little else. We soon realized we could not leave the baby in that hot, attic room or we might lose her, so when the grandparents offered to take the child and care for her, we accepted, though it was hard to give her up.

Rudy's boss had offered us a tiny storage room on the top floor of the factory as sleeping quarters, because the long train trip was difficult when Rudy had to work overtime. We accepted gratefully. Since the baby was in good hands, we could leave our chimney-attic room and the old farmhouse. We carried our few belongings to the city, furnishing our new room with two army cots and some boxes. We felt very fortunate.

After a few weeks of intense search, I found a job in a coat factory and was promoted to office work after a short time. With both of us working, we were soon able to buy ourselves bicycles and also pay the grandparents more for care of the baby. Every weekend we bicycled long miles to see our little daughter for a few short hours. Returning Sunday night, I would lie in bed unable to sleep, my heart aching with longing for my Christel. Again prayer helped relieve the loneliness and helped me to learn patience.

One thing that brightened my days were Mother's frequent letters. They were comfort and security—and they unlocked my memory fully, though many names and events had come back to me before I found her again.

At a time when we expected it least, Rudy was promoted from packer to be the new export manager. The pay was two and a half times what he had earned before, and a church member had just offered us a basement apartment in his house.

While Rudy began to build up his new export department from nothing, I began to set up our first real household the same way. Then came the happy day when we could bring our child home. She was two years old, and had never seen the city. After a few weeks of readjustment she was happy again and filled our lives with a new joy. She liked to go to church and impressed the women of the church with her model behaviour,

Christel was like her daddy—quiet, reserved, and gentle—and she became a favourite child to many. How proud we were to show her off!

Yes, things were brightening up for us. Later, Rudy found a little house for rent on the outskirts, close to the new plant the company was building. Christel's little brother had just arrived. With prayers of thankfulness we moved out of the city into that cute little house with its garden and big evergreen tree. The new baby had fresh air and sunshine, and Christel played for many hours beside his basket.

What a special moment it was when Mother at last came to visit me after our household was set up. Sepp, who didn't live far from us, had gone to bring her. He and I bickered from the minute she arrived about who had a greater right to keep her the longest! Of course, Sepp won out because he was the son —but Mother stayed with me long enough to tell me all that had happened since we had parted so many years before.

Father's illness had demanded several surgeries during the war, leaving him disabled and harder to live with than ever before. Mother nursed him patiently. When the Russians marched in, Father was on his deathbed. The Russians never molested Mother nor broke into the house to plunder. Father coughed continuously and the Russians assumed that he had TB, though it was not so, and they were afraid of his germs. He died of cancer.

The villagers helped Mother bury him at the old graveyard, and Mother was allowed to stay in her house for several months. Then came the time when even the Germans who had not belonged to the Nazi Party had to leave the village—Mother too. The people were penned for days in railway stock cars and finally arrived somewhere in East Germany. By then the East German government had erected some crude refugee shelters for those "privileged" refugees who were "politically clean," and Mother found herself in a hall on some straw for a place to lie down, and very much alone. The community spirit disintegrated and everyone fared for himself as survival became more crucial. It was the old story—no food for the refugees.

"I had managed up to that point," Mother said to me, "but that evening on the straw I felt hungry for the first time. The camp officials tried their best. We received a cup of very weak cereal coffee—plain—and they had a big white radish for each one of us. But, *Marichen*, I couldn't eat that coarse radish on my empty stomach. I tried but I just couldn't! I gave the radish to a teenage boy—he gobbled it down in a hurry—and I tried to go to sleep. I cried, *Marichen*, and I prayed! I said: "Lord, your Bible has a promise that assures your children of bread and water. I read it so often that those two things are certain for those who trust you. You did give me water tonight, dear Lord, but you didn't send bread. Only a radish, and my stomach couldn't handle that hot stuff. Please, Lord, all I want is a crust of plain bread, no fancy meal, just what you promised, *bread*, real bread!"

My heart cringed while listening to my aged little mother. I could see her there on that hard floor, on some smelly straw, all alone and helpless.

"I cried myself to sleep that night," Mother continued, "and when I awoke the next morning I reached automatically into my purse. You know it, girl, we refugees always held tight to our stuff even during our sleep because there was so much stealing going on everywhere. I checked to see that nothing had been stolen while I slept. Guess what I felt?"

I held my breath and didn't dare to say it.

"Bread," Mother confirmed; "a big crust of bread! I looked very nonchalantly into my purse so as not to draw attention to myself and then I began to eat, leaving the bread hidden. I broke off a little piece to still my hunger, but I didn't find out until weeks later who had given me the bread. Guess who did it?"

I shook my head. Who would give bread away at such a time?

"It was Octavian's wife. Do you remember her?"

Octavian's wife. Hadn't that been a neighbour of Mother's when I was a child? A rather unfriendly woman who poked fun at us for our religion? "What?" I said. "You must be joking, Mother."

Mother smiled. "She mellowed after Octavian died and we became good friends after the Russians marched in. We would sometimes stay together at night because we both lived alone and she would even urge me to pray for her. But she never could bring herself to the place to pray or accept God for her life. Well, that woman had still her golden wedding ring with her when we arrived that evening. And she went out in the night and found a farmer who exchanged a loaf of bread for her ring."

"And shared it with you? That's unbelievable, Mother. That's not possible!"

"God impressed her, she told me later, when she confessed her good deed to me. She said it was like someone gave her an order to break a piece off of that only bread she had and slip it into my purse during the night."

"What happened when you had used up the bread?"

"That is another miracle, my girl. We were only a few days in that Communist camp before we were loaded into the same railway cars and sent over the borderline into West Germany. There we were received with food and put into a pretty decent refugee camp. I never starved again, *Marichen*. From then on I always had some food that I could eat."

It was incredible. The Communists actually sent a whole train full of refugees over into the American zone of Germany when on the other hand they shot at anyone who tried to escape across no-man's-land to the West. They sent my mother's train to freedom, and we found each other! Was there anything too hard for God?

I never told Mother of the nightmares that I had about her on my flight. She would have scolded in her gentle way: "*Marichen*, how could you have doubted that God would take care of me? Are not all his promises 'yes' and 'amen'?"

I told her only a few things about my life. I didn't want to upset her. She always sounded so courageous when she told of her own hardships, but she couldn't bear the thought of her children's past suffering.

"Mother," I said, "remember the text in the Bible where it says that God loved us when we were his enemies?"

She nodded.

"God never left me, either, even when I hated Jesus. He went with me through labour camp and everything else!" Then I told her about the night when a voice told me not to go into the straw barn. Tears ran down her deeply wrinkled face as she listened.

"*Marichen*, I prayed for you during that time. I prayed for all of my children several times every day. I didn't know if any one of you were still alive or if I alone was left. I had not much hope that *you* had made it since you lived in Prague and we had heard of the murdering of Nazis, but I prayed for you anyhow!"

"I prayed for you"—it echoed in my heart. Mother prayed for me, and all at once I understood why I was still alive.

When Mother left again to visit Sepp, I felt less antagonistic towards his possessiveness. Mother would come back again some day and stay with me for a long time. I had her promise and the assurance of her love—and her prayers embraced me and my family though we had to part for a while.

Rudy's department had grown to such an extent that in the busy season he had eight people working under him. Rudy and

I had grown very active in the church and we held several church offices. We were on our way to becoming a respected family of the German middle class, and we could forget our humbling experiences and enjoy life. All was well with God and the world—except for my ulcers and the occasional little squabbles that any marriage has, and we had found an antidote for the latter.

"Let's pray together," one of us would say, reaching for the other's hand. Every evening, regardless if we felt mad, sad, or loving, we prayed and forgave. We knew that we were incompatible in many ways, but prayer kept us together and helped me to become more warm and responsive as a wife. I was determined to forget the shadows of my past and be the example of a Christian wife and mother, and I felt rather sure that I was well on my way.

Then out of the blue came a flash of lightning to my soul. An elderly church sister faced me one day after church. "Maria Anne," she said solemnly, "I wasn't aware that your father is still alive. I thought you grew up an orphan."

I felt defensive and uncomfortable. What was that all about? Sure, she was a dear friend of mine, but why would she start to pry into my past?

"Who told you about it?" I asked.

"Never mind that," she said soberly. "You have been on my mind the whole week because you told someone that you hated your father! I must talk to you about that!"

I frowned and waved my hands impatiently. "There is nothing to talk about. I have a right to resent my papa; he never cared for me and I hardly know him. I suppose he is still alive somewhere back in Czechoslovakia, but for me he is dead. I prefer to think of him that way." I waved good-bye and turned to leave.

"Maria Anne," the little old saint persisted, "the Bible says

'Honour your father and mother.' it doesn't say, 'Honour your *good* father.' "

I walked away without a word. There was a storm in my heart and I felt angry and insulted.

The nerve some people have, I thought. How could she dare to put her nose into my personal life and offer her saintly advice? How could she know how it felt to be forsaken by a parent?

My ulcers acted up so badly by the time my family and I arrived at home that I couldn't eat. I put my two children down for their afternoon naps and lay down myself. In the quiet of the bedroom I argued with God. I prayed, I accused, I cried. What was my problem?

And then it hit me like a thunderbolt. The Man on the cross! I had never faced up to him. From the time I decided it was only decent to serve God in return for all his kindness, until the present moment, I had simply exchanged allegiances and gods. As a child I had lived by my mother's God-concepts and tried to obey her; later I gave my loyalties to the *Führer*, worshipped him and obeyed his word. When I had become willing to acknowledge the sovereignty of the Great Ruler of the universe, I had served him mechanically, as all my life I had been taught to serve; I was now trying to earn my way to heaven. But I had never trusted the Jew from Nazareth as my personal Saviour!

Yes, I talked about Jesus; prayed to the Father in his name, read about him in my Bible, and confessed him. But he was far away in heaven and I was on earth, and I thought it good to keep that distance.

"Why, O God, why?" Why is it that I don't know you, Christ of the cross?"

In the quiet of my little bedroom, pain-racked by my stomach, I found some answers that afternoon.

I had heard about Jesus' life; I was talking about it. I thought it admirable, but I didn't want to live it—I couldn't!

There were two things I couldn't give up—my pride and my hate!

Not give up my pride? Hadn't I humbled myself willingly, down into the dust, ever since I joined a Christian church? Yes, and I was proud of it! How deceitful can the human heart be! I had accepted Christianity as if it were a change of garments —from the filthy rags of a social outcast to the cleaner church outfit of good works and better behaviour—but I had not sought Christ's robe of righteousness for my soul. How often religion is only an exchange of sins—from the coarse sins of immorality and arrogance to a respectable set which permits spiritual pride and anger under the cloak of lip service to Christ!

Yes, I knew why I had never been willing to come to terms with the Man on the cross—I had known it all along, but had never been willing to admit it! I would always just approach the cross, give it a short glimpse, and then run away because I could not stay and listen—listen to those words I was afraid to hear: "Father, forgive them, for they know not what they do." I couldn't face him under that crown of thorns, bleeding, hanging, while his words echoed to me through the centuries: "Love your enemies, do good to those who hate and despise you—"

"Son of God, I cannot do it! I cannot stop hating. I can only push it out of my memory and try to ignore it. And every time I think of it again my hands form a fist. Man on the cross, I cannot even understand why *you* let yourself be nailed to the cross. I would never, never let them do it to me if I had the power you did. Didn't you have any pride? Jesus, why didn't you just take a bolt of lightning and knock them all out? Wipe them out, those miserable creatures! Oh, how I hate meanness and cruelty, and how I hate your persecutors and mine: that Czech overseer, those Russian soldiers who hurt my Helga. Jesus Christ, I am afraid of you! You're asking me to love my enemies, and I can't even have kind thoughts towards my father. God, you're asking the impossible of me—and I fear you, God! I can serve you in fear and give you due honour, but I don't know how to love. Christ, I am even afraid to love you. You might ask me to become like you; but I can't! Pride and hate are part of me. I will crumble if I let go of them!"

I felt better for having been honest with myself and God. But there was no hope left in me. I knew myself and I would have to live with it—that was all.

# 17
# *Jesus, My Friend*

A few days later my aunt came from East Germany for a visit. She was the unmarried older sister of my own mother. She and I didn't know each other, but I felt it my duty to look after her; she was all alone. So Rudy went and got her, and I regretted it from the first hour she arrived.

We couldn't get along together. Maybe we were too much alike. Maybe I was on edge because I had lost contact with God. She was very religious and lived by the Bible teachings—but mainly the "thou shalt not" admonitions. Her "don'ts" were our daily bread but they made neither of us the better because both of us were worried about my sick soul.

I came down with the "grippe" and it was a relief. I had to stay in bed where she couldn't preach to me. I was sick for a few days and my recovery was slow. I felt bored, restless, and impatient to get up and take over my household again. Who knew what that peculiar old aunt would do to my children when I wasn't around!

My eyes fell on a little black book on my nightstand. Auntie had put it there shortly after she arrived and admonished me to read it. Of course, I wouldn't. Not in a million years. I felt much too rebellious towards her to do her that favour.

But I was so bored and time ticked by so slowly—it would be hours before Rudy would be home to talk to. What was that book about, anyway? It had an unusual title: *Die Quelle der Kraft* (The Wellspring of Power). It was a translation from the English, entitled *Alone with God,* written by an American missionary, Matilda Erickson Andross. Oh—from America! That made me less resentful towards the book.

America! Though I knew almost nothing about it, the word had a good sound to my ears. Only three times in my life had I met Americans. First was that morning when I had run by accident into that American barracks after crossing no-man's-land, and I would never forget those unknown American soldiers' kindness. My heart always felt warm when I remembered how they had helped us. The second time I had faced an American was when I was the principal in my little country school and we had been ordered to attend a district meeting. An American educator had talked to us about democracy. He had the cutest accent speaking German, and I listened carefully. After his speech he offered to answer questions. I had several, but I was much too nervous and afraid to speak up before a crowd of people.

One male teacher stood up and said: "Whenever you referred to our German past or the philosophy of Nazi education, you sounded very hesitant. You acted like the cat walking around the hot mash."

The teachers in the audience smiled. The American guest speaker seemed a bit uneasy. "The reason for that is that I tried not to hurt your feelings. It has been only such a short time since you all taught under Hitler. I fully understand if you still feel very much as you did during Nazi times—it will take time to reorient your thinking towards democratic principles!"

I found myself standing and my heart was throbbing in my throat, but I had to answer him. "Sir," I said, and took a deep breath, "if you try to indicate that we are still Nazis, you are wrong. We are not Nazis nor anything else. We trusted once and paid with our heart blood for it. We got hurt, sir, and we are still hurting, and we are not willing to trust again—neither democracy nor any other system. So it isn't that we are against what you said; it just sounds too good to be true, at least for us, for we are like burned children who are afraid of fire!"

Applause rippled and I looked around to see for whom the applause was meant. It finally dawned on me that my fellow teachers applauded my words, and I sat down, terribly embarrassed.

The American speaker found me after the meeting and shook my hand and thanked me for what I had said. His obvious willingness to respect my view left me puzzled—what made Americans tolerant with people of other convictions? I did not know the spirit of tolerance; it wasn't a meaningful word in my vocabulary.

The third time I faced an American was when an agent from the Central Intelligence Agency came to our basement shortly after we had brought our Christel home. We had applied through a church agency for a sponsor so we could emigrate to the United States of America, and the agent came to tell us that there was no chance for us—records about our past stood in the way as Rudy had engaged in direct warfare against the United States.

That was a dark hour in our life, and I had prayed and hoped for a miracle, but I had consoled myself—maybe God didn't want us to leave Germany.

And now I held a religious book written by an American woman. I glanced at the first page, and her style caught me from the first sentence. She wrote as simply as that American lecturer spoke when he explained democracy to us, and it fascinated me!

There was nothing of the fancy vocabulary and rhetoric I was accustomed to from German literature, lectures, and sermons.

She explained it so simply that even my children could have understood, but her simplicity did not offend me, though I prided myself about my use of a wide vocabulary at all times. The simplicity of her book disarmed me in leading me like a child to see Jesus.

I had never thought of him as a friend but as a God and King to pay homage to. He was a Judge whom I would face (and I dreaded it). But this writer said Christ had all heaven waiting for us to bring special blessing into our lives. He had only thoughts of peace for us and great plans to use us in a mighty way if we could learn *one* thing: how to communicate with him. It was a book on prayer, and I wondered what she meant. I knew how to pray. Twice a day I knelt down and talked to God, always very thoughtful not to forget to give thanks first before I asked God for help, protection, and other gifts; always very careful to be reverent, respectful, and to use the proper vocabulary.

This writer said there was nothing wrong with a formal prayer, but Christ longed for more than that!

She likened communication with Jesus to a telephone conversation—we on one end, he listening on the other. But the usual prayers of Christians were monologues, she said. We would say our piece, finish with "Amen," and slam the receiver down. Shouldn't we stop long enough to listen? Would not Christ talk back to us if we waited for an answer? The thought of it nearly overwhelmed me—but she quoted several famous people of British and American church history who acknowledged that Christ had talked to them, and it all sounded so terribly simple! She quoted Scripture texts such as "My sheep hear my voice". Christ the great Shepherd said it, and I wondered if I were his sheep. One sentence, however, hammered into my mind above everything else, and I repeated it over and over until tears flowed and I couldn't see the pages: "Jesus and I are friends!"

How simple, how beautiful, how unbelievable!

Jesus and I are friends! How I wanted to be able to say the same, but that was impossible. She was good, had been a missionary and a servant of God. Of course Christ would be *her* friend. But he would never stoop to be *my* personal friend; I had been his enemy and I was still a rebel in my heart—proud, hateful. He would never answer if I listened; or would he?

I finished the book, and when Rudy came home I asked him to move my cot out to the balcony of our little house. It was a warm night and he consented. I liked to sleep under the stars; it made me always so still inside and so small, and God seemed nearer than during the day.

Lying on my bed, I began to talk to him. It took courage because I wondered if he would be offended if I didn't kneel down, but I did it anyway.

"Jesus," I said in my heart, "I want you as a friend, but I am not so sure that I am good enough to be talked to by you. The book says that it doesn't matter how I feel; you can change me, even my pride and hate, if I let you—I just give you my will and that's all. But I understand if you can't talk to me, Jesus, because I turned so much against you as a Nazi."

"I love you, my child, and I have called you by your name," an inner voice answered.

I sat bolt upright. "God," I said softly, "*did* you speak to me, or was it just my own heart? Please God, don't let anything or anybody speak again if it is not you, dear Jesus; I am afraid I am making a fool of myself!"

"You are mine," he said; "don't be afraid. I died for you and I have called you to serve me. You shall do great things for me!"

"O Jesus," I said into the night, tears streaming down my cheeks, "I don't deserve so much love and I can't see how I ever could do anything great for you. You know I am a human wreck, ulcers, nerves, and all. But Jesus, what's left of me is *yours.* Even my bad feelings and my horrible memories. I give you all there is to give. Just be my friend and talk to me sometimes; that's all I want for the rest of my life!"

Jesus and I became friends that night when I surrendered my all to him the best I knew how. Not that surrendering to Christ is over in a moment. When a human being gives himself to Christ, it is the beginning of eternity, and it becomes a more meaningful reality from day to day with no end to its depth.

I wasn't a new person when I got up the next morning: it was still painracked, tired me, and my feelings had not changed. I couldn't love Papa even if I tried. I couldn't forgive those Russians and I wasn't sure I should. There was just one difference: I had found a Friend to talk to every time I needed to talk, and he would talk back if I listened, and I could stop worrying about all my weakness since it was now his problem, not mine.

"Jesus," I said before I went to church, "if that saint talks to me about my papa, what do I say?"

"Don't worry about it; everything will change, be patient," my Lord comforted.

"Lord, change my hate to love," I begged every day. But it took a long time. Some people may change in the twinkling of an eye; I was obviously too stubborn for such a miracle.

My attitudes changed very slowly from hate to pity, from pity to compassion. God is in no hurry.

My aunt still irked me, but I had someone to talk to about it, so I didn't answer her back so much, and we discovered one great love we had in common: Jesus Christ.

How can people fight when they talk about Jesus? How can people hate when they feel sorry for those who don't know the Lord?

It came so naturally; I had nothing to pretend and to force when I sat down one day to write to Papa. My aunt knew his address.

"Dear Papa, you are much on my mind lately, and there are some rumours that your wife is dying of cancer and that you have a lady friend and two children by her.

"I want you to know that I am sorry that I treated you so unkindly. Please forgive me!

"We as a family have never been together on this earth. I wish so much that we could live together in eternity.

"Papa, I long so much for you to know my Jesus. He loves you and is waiting for you. Don't worry that you were his enemy all your life. I was, too, but Jesus took me as his own. He will do the same for you. I love you, Papa! Your daughter, Maria."

I never would have dreamed that my papa could write such a warm letter back as he did. The old bitter Herr Appelt had mellowed, and he corroborated the gossip that he had two small children. One was a little boy named Rudy after the Navy man I had loved so much during the war. The girl was Angelika because she looked like a little angel.

Letters flew back and forth, and I watched a miracle unfold from beginning to end.

God's timing is always perfect. With my first letter God sent a man into Papa's home—a retired minister of the gospel from the church my father fought so bitterly when he was newly married to my mother. Papa became friends with that man of God. So did his girlfriend. They both accepted Christ and wondered what to do next. According to the Bible they lived in adultery. Papa got a divorce and married the mother of the children. Then they longed to share their new faith with the dying Czech woman Papa divorced.

They nursed her and cared for her and the children brightened her last days, but she was too bitter to accept God. She died angry. Papa's letters were filled with deep anguish—oh, to undo life's great mistakes, but so often it is too late, too late!

We comforted each other, for Christ forgives even if our own heart condemns us.

It was so good to see Papa safe in God's hand—him and his family. One great question I still had in my mind was what my Lord had said to me that night under the stars when I found him: "You shall do great things for me!"

What did God mean by that? I couldn't do anything special for him ever. My education was of no use. I was sick; we were relatively poor. The greatest thing I longed to do was to lead someone to Christ. But I had never been able to find anyone who would want to accept my Jesus except for Papa and his new wife, and it was really that minister who had led them to the cross.

"Lord, will I ever find a soul for you?" I said over and over. But no one seemed interested though I tried to witness. Maybe I didn't know how.

Every autumn our church had *Erntedank* (harvest-thanks). Charity towards the poor and needy was greatly encouraged. In order to do more, church members were provided with stacks of Thanksgiving magazines and asked to go out and sell them, since soliciting is forbidden in Germany. The money went for disaster relief.

Selling magazines was not our cup of tea, so Rudy and I always paid for the magazines ourselves and gave them away. We did so for several years.

Now harvest time had come around again and the magazines were in our arms to take home.

"Jesus," I said when we arrived at home after church, "do we *have* to sell these magazines this year, or can we handle it the usual way."

"You better go out and sell them," my Lord said.

"I was afraid you would say that, Lord," I sighed. "Where do you want us to sell them?"

"In your own street, here on Weisspfennig Weg," God said.

"Lord, this *isn't* your voice talking to me. That is the devil's, isn't it? You don't want us to go in our own street, Lord, please. None of them are Protestant, and they think us strange as it is. After all, Lord, we have to live with our neighbours. Please don't ask us to make life more difficult!"

"Go in your own street," the voice said, and it was a clear order.

"You better convince Rudy, then," I said. "He won't like it!"

Rudy didn't like the idea at all. He hated to do any selling, but he finally agreed to go with me. We each took one side of the street, and the magazines sold fast. Soon we were done and were very relieved and pleased about our success.

We turned our money in and felt at peace with God and the world again. But who should come to us after church but my saintly, elderly friend and hand us a pack of magazines.

"What's this?" I frowned.

"Listen, I paid for those magazines." She nodded her hoary head proudly. "But I'll *give* you the magazines to sell and you can keep the money to buy food for your love gifts to East Germany and Czechoslovakia."

She was so sincere and so sure that she was doing me a favour. I had no choice but to smile and give her a warm "Thank you." Rudy groaned softly after we were out of her sight. I couldn't help smiling about the way God was driving home a lesson.

"Fine, Lord," I said and felt good. "So you want us to do double duty this year to make up for the last lean years of service. You win, Jesus. We'll go. But where?" It was no problem any more, I didn't mind going anywhere, and our own block was done.

"Go in your own street."

I hadn't heard right. Or was someone mocking me?

"Jesus," I said urgently, "I am not playing make-believe; I

really believed that you were talking to me. But that is not your order. You wouldn't forget that we went there last week!"

"Go in your own street," the Lord insisted.

"Lord, do you mean our Weisspfennig Weg?"

"Yes. Go in your own street!"

I sighed. "Lord, how do I explain *that* to my husband?"

There was no other explanation and I felt utterly bewildered.

Rudy raised his eyebrows while I stuttered my story to him.

"Honey," he said kindly, "the people bought already. They'll think we're nuts."

I nodded. I knew all that, but I either believed it to be God's order or not. And I wanted to believe it.

Rudy decided to act funny about it all, since I was just about on the brink of tears.

"Okay, let's switch sides. I take your side; you take the one I sold last week. At least the people will not know what's up!"

That relieved my embarrassment a little and we went out.

It was just as I expected. Nobody bought and I found myself at the end of my side waiting for Rudy. By then I was sure I was off my rocker and I would never expect an answer from the Lord again.

Rudy came after a long while and I was more irritated because of the delay.

He beamed! "Schatzi, did you get into that house last week?" He pointed to a fenced-in, two-storey apartment house at the end of the street.

"No, the gate was locked and a big dog was in the yard, and I was out of magazines, too!"

"Well, that's why we had to repeat our selling with switched sides, Maria Anne. For in that house lives a couple who need Christ!"

"You believe that God told us to go again?"

"I do now. I actually went to make you feel better; you seemed so upset. But now I see God's hand. You see, I got into the apartment house when someone walked out as I tried to get in. And I am not afraid of harmless little dogs!" Rudy winked at me. "I sold some, but at last I found a door in the attic and knocked. A woman opened the door a few centimetres and started to talk to me. She bought a magazine and invited us to come back when her husband is home. She once was a church member, but her husband is against religion, and she warned me not to push it upon him, or he would get violent!"

"What makes you think that they're interested in Christ?"

"I didn't say that. I believe they *need* Christ!"

I couldn't object to that, and we went back for a visit later when the husband was home.

Hans and Frieda were a lovely, elderly, childless couple. Hans shot questions at us as fast as we could answer in return. The conversation had *one* theme—God and religion. Frieda sat and stared at her husband. He seemed eager, overeager to talk about God.

When we left after long hours of deep talk, he took us to the gate and shook our hands.

"Please do come back soon, friends," he said, and there were tears in his friendly eyes. "I have waited for you for six months." Noticing our surprised looks, he hastened to explain. "You see, I felt for a long time that it was time to make peace with God and I asked him—" he pointed to the sky—"to send someone to explain things to me. I am a simple labourer who doesn't know how to figure things out. God finally sent you. I had almost given up hope!"

We assured him that we would be back and then we walked to our home silently. We both had much to think about.

"I am sorry, Jesus, that I doubted your orders!" I could picture my Lord smiling and I smiled back.

Yes, Hans and Frieda were the first persons we led to Christ. They joined the church, became our most devoted friends, and Hans became a church elder. Frieda died a few years later, but Hans kept that newfound joy. "I'll see her again," he said, and squeezed our hands. He was so grateful to us.

Yes, Christ's words to me had come true. I had been a tool in his hand to do "great things" and I was satisfied. Now I could relax, enjoy the abundant life, and rest in him. My cup was running over.

# And the Sequel

The propellers droned on in the black night, and the ocean below us like the shrouded stars above could only be suspected.

That I was sitting in an airplane on my way to America was only a dream—something I had dreamed so often that finally it seemed real to me—or was it?

My six-year-old Christel and little Michael slept in their seats; so did Rudy. To the left of me sat an old woman dozing —while her fingers held tightly to a rosary twisted around her wrist. Poor little woman! She was so afraid of flying, petrified by the thought of being above deep waters which could swallow her if the plane had to go down. I had to admit that it wasn't too comforting a thought, but I wasn't afraid. It couldn't happen! God hadn't opened a door for us to the New World after so many years just to let us drown before we entered. Neither would he let the old mother beside me die before she saw her daughter in New York again and had a few wonderful years of a new life in that great land. God is love, and he has thoughts of peace for his children and great plans for all of us—for everyone in this chartered plane for that matter, since all of us were emigrants to the United States of America!

What a whirlwind the last few months had been. Just at the

time when I had finally resigned myself to the fact that we were not supposed to take off to a new land but find our home in Germany, our papers had come through in spite of our past records. A sponsor had been found by friends who had left the previous year for that land of promise, and here we were, free like birds and ready for a great new future.

What a blessing that things had turned so fast for us, or we would have never got away at all. I still couldn't understand why everyone had tried so hard to discourage us from going. Though it was good to have so many friends who hated to see us go, and I could understand why Rudy's parents resented it, we were not leaving for good. We were just going to America to get ourselves better trained for God's ministry, then we would return.

I had never seen my foster mother so upset—ever—as when we visited her a few days before our plane left. Just thinking of it made me heartsick again.

Our furniture and belongings had all been given away. There were enough poor refugees around us who needed everything we had accumulated since Rudy's promotion at work. We had kept only two suitcases full of wordly possessions: the big suitcase had the clothing for our family of four. The smaller case was heavy like lead and full of books—the only thing I had not been willing to part with was our books. Books to me had always been like friends. They could be shared, but never discarded.

With our two children and the two suitcases, we had made our rounds in southern Germany to say good-bye to our loved ones. The last stop was my mother. We went to church together for the first time since I had left the little cottage as a young girl to go to Prague. I didn't let go of her hand while we shared the Lord's supper, sang hymns, and knelt for our last prayer together. The parting was that painful and frustrating.

"God just gave you back to me after all those years of un-certainty and praying, *Marichen.* Why do you want to leave me now again to go so far away?"

Mother's voice was only a whisper; her breath was so short and laboured from her fluttering, weak heart, and her thin lips now had a shiny tinge of blue.

"Mother," I said, trying to hold back tears, "I don't want to leave you. You know how much I love to be around you. But I am sure that Jesus wants us to go to the other land. It is his will, Mother."

"If it is, then I must let you go, *Marichen,*" Mother said, nodding gently. "But are you sure you are doing his will? You could be running ahead of God, my girl, because you *want* to go to America; it is easy to call our own desires God's will, and you have always been very headstrong and im-patient!'

"Mother," I said, tortured, "we prayed so much about it. It *is* God's will—and even if we were mistaken it's too late now. We burned our bridges behind us!"

It was again a train that took me away from her. But this time there was peace in my mother's face, and in the clatter-ing of the wheels I called: "Mother, wait for me, I am coming back to you!' She did not answer, but just waved and cried and I tried to smile.

Now I listened to the night song of the propellers as the plane flew west, and my soul was troubled.

What if Mother was right? What if our move was not God's will and we had run ahead of him? Would Christ go with me if I was going my own way? I looked back east where home had been, and my heart called for comfort.

"Are you still with me, Lord? Or have you left me, in case we misunderstood you? Where are you, Jesus?"

The eastern sky began to glow, and light stretched out her fingers to touch the night while I listened.

"Fear not, for I have redeemed you; I have called you by your name; you are mine! When you pass through the waters, I will be with you, and through the rivers, they shall not overflow you; when you walk through the fire you shall not be burned, neither shall the flame kindle upon you" (Isaiah 43:1, 2).

"What a strange text to give to me, Jesus, to begin our new life with." Why should there be fire and water and deep rivers? Weren't we just about ready to enter the land of great opportunities, the land of milk and honey, the promised land of my dreams?

"That's the Statue of Liberty," Rudy said as our plane swept low to land. I hadn't time to look because my children complained of nausea, and the old woman beside me prayed aloud in her fright. I held her hand very tight and smiled reassurance to Chris.

"We are almost in America!" I said. The date was May 5, 1955.

An hour later on that special day in May, I found myself sitting at the railway terminal in New York City awaiting a train to Michigan where our sponsor lived. I was dumbfounded, shocked, and frightened.

Was *this* America? Oh, no, that was impossible! The place was horrible, dirty, full of dumped newspapers, beer cans, and other garbage. Didn't a rich country like this have enough pride to keep a place up? And the people! Why did they dump stuff? Weren't they proud of America? Didn't they care?

Didn't they care about each other? There were so many people rushing or just sitting around, but nobody ever nodded or smiled. And their attire! How shocking!

Didn't Americans know how to dress for travel? After all, this *was* a terminal and people came here for that purpose.

Oh, some people looked proper for the occasion, but most of them looked sloppy—like the station. And there were so many old people, mostly men, sitting on benches. They didn't even have suitcases or bags. They just sat and stared, looking as poor as German refugees, even unshaved, ungroomed.

One woman walked by, dragging a child. She wore short pants and no stockings. What a shocking way to appear in public, I thought.

My children nestled close to me. They were overtired and afraid. Since we had to wait for several hours, Rudy had left us to explore New York, and I felt helpless.

What a strange language. I hadn't thought of that before we left. I didn't understand a single syllable. Where did I have my dumb head? Just because I had grown up bilingual and always managed to communicate enough to get by—even with the Russians—I hadn't realized how different English was. And now, for the first time that I could remember, I knew not one word to read or speak. Our departure had come so fast I didn't have time to prepare myself at all.

An elderly gentleman sat down on our bench. I moved the suitcases closer to me and held tight to the children.

"Are you new in this land?" a voice said in German, and I looked up. The man smiled. I was so relieved to hear my own tongue that I fought tears.

"How did you know, sir?" I asked, smiling gratefully.

"You three look different and very lonely," the man said. "New York people don't wear winter coats in May when it is 70 degrees. Where are you from?"

Glad that someone understood me, I talked unafraid. I even expressed my surprise about the dirt and that it all seemed so different, so uncultured, so to speak!

"May I give you some advice?" the old man asked.

I nodded eagerly.

"You will find this land altogether different than you expected it, *junge Frau*, but learn to say nothing until your first shock is over. Americans thrive on criticizing their own land but they resent it when others do it. Remember, it's *different*, not worse, than Europe—as different as the moon from the earth. Learn to accept the difference and your children will have a better future than you do!

I thanked the man for his kind advice and turned to Michael who stood before me making significant gestures. Oh, dear, *now* what would I do?

"What's the matter, lady, is something wrong?" The old man was kind.

"Oh," I said and burst into tears. "I know so little about English that I can't even find a toilet for the little fellow— and my husband is not around to help me out. He knows English."

"Well, you'll learn fast; don't worry. Go to those doors over there and look for W-O-M-E-N." He spelled the letters out in the German way. "That's the place for you and your little boy. I will stay here and watch your cute little daughter and your luggage."

I was apprehensive, but needn't have been. He was friendly, did as he said, and talked to me for a long time before he wished us luck and walked away into the crowd.

It didn't dawn on me until later that God had sent that stranger just at the right moment. I took his advice to heart and it saved us much trouble.

There was so much that was different for us that I sometimes had to bite my lips not to speak up.

When we finally arrived at our sponsor's place, even Rudy was flabbergasted. They were an elderly couple and he was in the construction business. They had a large house at the outskirts of the town and they had prepared one bedroom for us.

"Mary," the lady of the house said, and Rudy translated, "I hope the closet is big enough for you four. I have so much stuff in the other bedrooms I couldn't give you any more space to unpack."

"It's more than enough," Rudy said politely and gave me the word. I looked at him.

"Rudy, why do two people have that much stuff?"

Ludwig, the sponsor, overheard me, and he still understood some German since his parents had come from Germany.

"Tell your wife that it is hopeless. My wife is a hoarder and the only solution to our problem is a good fire. Wait until you see our garage. We have to park the cars outside—the junk is accumulating that much!" The big man laughed; my blank look amused him.

I looked blanker yet when I saw him step into his car to drive down to his mailbox, about a hundred yards from the house.

"We are lazy, Mary," he said. "I know I should walk, but Americans don't have their legs for walking, just to sit down!"

I guessed what he said in his German-English mixture and nodded. I had given up trying to understand reasons; I was glad enough just to make sense out of the words.

The first three words that made a lasting impression on my receptive mind were "dollars", "sale", and "diet". I picked those words out in an early conversation, and I got their meaning very fast but not their connection for a while.

Emilie, the sponsor's wife, took us to the grocery store the day after our arrival. It was a large supermarket and I had never seen anything like it.

"Rudy," I said, "ask her what people do with so much food. Doesn't it spoil?"

Rudy translated. She smiled. "Oh, there are many more stores in the big city, bigger than this market. Americans eat a lot."

That made sense, because both of our sponsor's frames were

very well padded. She was much shorter than I was but at least twice as far around, and maybe double my weight.

"Tell your wife that Americans have to go on diets very often to lose weight," she continued.

"Vat is diet?" I tried to speak English.

"The reduction of the daily calorie intake down to one thousand calories a day," the fat lady said with a sigh. "I know I have to go on a diet again. So does Lue. The doctor said so."

Rudy explained. I sighed, too. What a strange land. I remembered we had been on ration cards in the American military zone of West Germany on 1200 calories per day (and often much less) for far too long. I could feel for her. But why do it in America with so much food around?

I followed Emilie's shopping cart. Michael sat on the cart, and Christel held tight to my hand, and we watched the lady pick her groceries. She would look around and always dart to some areas which had special signs: "Sale".

"What is s-a-l-e?" I asked Rudy in German. He asked her and she said something even Rudy couldn't follow, except that she used the word "dollars" and "cheaper" a lot.

By the time she was through shopping, I had learned the meaning of two words. "Sale" meant sweet stuff and toilet paper, and "diet" was the opposite of sale. For she had bought ice cream, candies, chocolate, marshmallows, jelly and toilet paper on sale, but not much low calorie stuff. Nor had she bought fruit, though Michael had reached for it. My children were not used to sweets, but loved apples and bananas. In Germany we had never been able to afford to buy as many as we wanted. We would buy *one* banana as a treat for all four of us.

"No," Emilie said to Michael when he reached for a banana. "They're too expensive. Wait till they're on sale."

Michael looked disappointed, and Rudy explained to me.

"But Rudy," I said, flustered, "she bought a whole box of

chocolate which isn't as good, much more expensive even on sale, and less healthful than bananas. Ask her."

Rudy didn't want to and we helped to carry several bags of groceries out. But I felt helpless when it came to putting the stuff away. Every cupboard was already full and the refrigerator was stuffed.

Ludwig saw my bewildered look. "Don't worry, Mary," he said in German, "my wife is very thrifty. She never throws left-overs away. She puts it into the refrigerator until it rots, and then she empties the refrigerator."

That made less sense than the "sale" and I felt so ignorant by then that I went into the privacy of our little bedroom and had a good cry.

All I wanted to do at any time was cry anyway! I was so homesick and hot and sticky and lost most of the time. All I could think was that I wanted to go home. So did my children, who refused to speak English. Maybe even Rudy wanted to go, though he tried to act enthusiastic.

Rudy worked as a carpenter's helper for Lue, and had a hard time. He had never done such work, never handled an electric saw, never hammered a nail, never worked in moist summer heat.

Rudy was a perfectionist; he had never done sloppy work in his life. But Lue was a businessman. Time was money. What did it matter if a board was nail crooked? It mattered to Rudy. One day he was so tense and nervous that the electric saw slipped out of his hands and he reached for it, afraid that the tool might fall and break and that would mean loss of money for us. The saw cut into the bone of his hand, and Rudy was rushed to a doctor.

For the first time we experienced what it meant to live without socialized medicine and sick day compensation—a must in all of Germany.

I went to work so we could pay our rent—ten dollars a week for the bedroom we lived in.

The only jobs I found were strawberry picking and house cleaning. I did both, and we were never behind in our bills.

Rudy's hand healed and he went back to work, but our sponsors felt they needed the privacy of their own home, so Emilie rented a small basement appartment for us.

The apartment consisted of a bedroom and a kitchen. Shower and bathroom facilities had to be shared by four families. Lue acted embarrassed when he came to visit us.

"Don't stay in there," he said. "It's no good."

I shook my head. "It's okay; don't worry, we'll make out." I had no smile left, and Lue walked to his car.

But it was not okay, and I knew it. But what could we do? I had never heard of a slum until I lived in it, and by then nothing could astonish me any more. I lived in a nightmare again, and waited to wake up—wake up in my little house in Germany where it was cool and smelled clean and where Rudy would come home on his bicycle from the office. But I never woke up. The horrible dream went on and on and on. Every morning when I got up to fix Rudy's lunch box, I got angry at the thick red dust on the old table. The same dust covered the outside of the tiny, lone window, high above the stove, and made it all dark so I couldn't see the sun and the sky beyond the basement entrance. I washed and dusted and rubbed to fight all the dirt, but it was hopeless because of the nearby highway, and I knew it.

I knew also that the highway was one reason Rudy looked so dreadfully tired. The big trucks shook the whole basement as they roared past the house and Rudy couldn't sleep with that noise. He was such a light sleeper and there were so many trucks on the road every night—every miserable, hot, and smelly night.

One night I was awake, too, and I got up to get a glass of

water. As I pulled the string to the dim light bulb that was in a shaky socket above the sink, I saw a movement, some beady eyes, and a fat rat's tail. I choked on the water and threw up into the sink. Rudy came out and asked what was the matter.

"Rudy, did I see what I think I did?" I asked, and my stomach convulsed again. "Are there rats in this basement?"

Rudy nodded and held me tight. Yes, he had known it since we had moved in, but he had never mentioned it since he knew my abhorrence of rats. I sobbed on his shoulder and begged, "Please, Rudy, take me home again. I can't stand it any longer. We have made a dreadful mistake. God has forsaken us and we are doomed if we stay here. We all will die. The kids have lost their smiles and are so pale. You are getting thinner and more exhausted every day and I—oh, Rudy, I am afraid I am pregnant again! What shall we do, Rudy? Where shall we go?"

Rudy took me back to bed and I cried myself to sleep in his arms. Rudy had black circles under his eyes when he left for work the next morning and he looked so haggard and aged. I felt guilty for having added to his burdens. He was so uncomplaining and brave, and so very quiet. He said less and less.

What was there to say? We both knew it all too well. We couldn't go back to Germany. We had no money and hadn't even finished paying back our fare to America to the World Church Service. We did send a few dollars every week from Rudy's small pay cheque—Lue didn't believe in overpaying people.

I couldn't go to work because there was no one to tend the children. But I cleaned some rich peoples' houses once a week. They allowed me to bring my children with me. But our combined earnings were just enough to make ends meet. We were not able to save anything.

Christel and Michael always stayed very close to me. They acted like two forlorn little birds, and Christel refused to go outside to play. She hated the grassless red dirt around the apartment house and the traffic close by, and would hide her face in my apron.

"*Mutti,* when will we go back home?" she would ask in her quiet way, and her big brown eyes would wait for an answer, but there was no answer. I would look up to that tiny, dark glass where there was supposed to be the sky, and I would call for my Lord, but there was no more answer, either, since I expected none. Somewhere I had lost contact with my faith, my home, and my smile. All I had left was a little pride. I tried to keep that rats' hole as clean as I could and I never wrote back to Germany that America was rats, dirt, and loneliness. I always managed vague, general letters. Maybe it wasn't even pride. Maybe I couldn't bear the thought of how they would worry about us. Maybe I was afraid to dishonour my God. We had been so sure that we had followed his guidance, and told everyone who had tried to tell us not to leave that it was God's will for us to go to America.

But it was a mistake, Lord, wasn't it? You didn't talk to me; it was only my eager heart that fooled me, and now all four of us had to pay the consequences for a faith that had been presumptuous. But *why* did we make that mistake, Lord? Why?

As long as it seemed we had followed God's leading to this strange land, I could endure almost anything. But if he had not led us . . . if we were here alone . . . if I had made a tragic mistake about hearing his voice . . .? At this point my morale hit an all-time low.

Now, as I remember those dark days, I wonder how I could have forgotten one of my favourite adages about life—the great truth that the darkest hour of every night is always just before the birth of a new morning? I had first realized this fact during those terrifying, sleepless nights of horror in the Communist labour camp. Some of those long-ago, pitch-black nights had clouded my spirit so deeply that I couldn't even imagine a new morning any more. It had seemed that black fear and hiding would go on forever—but then I had not known Jesus.

Now, though I knew him, darkness threatened to swallow me up again; I couldn't see even one ray of hope, and I forgot that my Bible called Jesus the bright morning star.

But though I couldn't see his light just then, he was near; I know it now. Once again we were students in God's school, learning hard but important lessons for our future service.

First, he wiped away all our unrealistic, fairy-tale dreams about the New World. Our minds were saturated with too many glowing stories about fortunate immigrants to this country who had "struck it rich" in a short time, and had settled down to a life of plenty and ease.

It did not take me long to find out that even in America, *Glückspilze* (lucky dogs) are few, compared with the many thousands of people who struggle their way out of poverty, slums, despair, and disillusionment just as we were having to do it—by willingness to do any kind of hard work that was available—a long, slow process!

Not for the first time (or the last) we observed how perfect is God's timing. He is never in a hurry, never early, never late. And he fulfils his plans in such a way that we can see later why he had to chasten us.

Step by step we edged our way into the mainstream of American life and into a new day.

There were friends whose lives inspired us deeply during that difficult period. One of these was *Tante* (Auntie) Erhard, as my children called her. She had been born in Russia, but her mother tongue was German. Her life story sounded stranger than fiction. She and her husband had remained faithful to Christianity in Communist Russia. Her husband had been drafted by the German army to become an interpreter, since he spoke Russian and German; close to the end of the war he broke away from the German troops and found the address of his wife and son in a German refugee camp in Poland. On the way to that camp the Russians snatched him and brought him before a Communist tribunal for treason: he was sentenced to labour camp in Siberia—at least, that's what reliable reports rumoured to *Tante* Erhard.

"Mary," she said to me, "I gave birth to my second son during those days, and shortly after his birth we were loaded into open cattle trucks to be transported to Germany because the Russians were pushing the frontline towards the West. It was in the deepest winter and we had no food or heat on the train. We rolled and were pushed around for days, and so many people died. The winds were murderous. Children froze stiff. Babies became like boards. The frozen bodies were just shoved out through the opening of the moving cattle trucks as we rolled on. My new baby had no chance, but I told God that I had dedicated both of my sons to him and he could take care of us.

"I laid my baby on my warm bare breasts under my clothes, and kept my other son under my big coat. Then I waited. It was just a matter of time before my milk would dry up and I would not be able to nurse any more, since we had no food nor water. For three days while the train rolled and the winds howled, I waited and prayed. My breasts never emptied, Mary, and my baby never got cold or hungry. We arrived in another camp in Germany where I could take care of my sons. We had the bare necessities. After the war ended we came to the United States, and here I work for my boys. Someday, Mary, someday they will serve God. He saved them for a purpose!"

I looked at her worn face and hands. She cleaned houses and did all sorts of odd jobs. They were as poor as we were, but what a spirit she had!

"As for my husband," she said, "something in my heart tells me that he is still alive. Someday I will hear from him again."

Poor *Tante* Erhard, I thought. She had no word from him

for the last eleven years; wasn't she just fooling herself with wishful thinking?

"As for you, Mary, stop wishing all the time to go back home to the old country. We older folks might never amount to much over here, but think of the children. They'll have a better life and a future. They can get an education and serve God someday. It's worth all the struggle and misery; just wait and see!"

Her courage helped to provide the lift I so much needed.

1962 found us in California.and after all those hard years of weariness and wandering it looked is if the time had finally come when we would be permitted to settle down. Rudy had a secure job with promotions ahead, and I found work in the local schools as a substitute teacher. We discovered a charming older home, large enough for our family—which now numbered seven. It was "on sale" (how well I knew that magic word by now!) so we bought it—and I planted a rose garden. Wasn't Jesus wonderful. Our lives were full of California sunshine and laughter and picnics.

Occasional clouds darkened the sun, like my major stomach surgery or when my beloved mother died before I could go back to Germany to see her as I had promised. It took me a long time to pull out of that shock.

"Why, Lord, why did you let her die before I could get to her?" I cried until there were no tears left in me and my heart was too numb to ache. Little by little, I was able to hear Jesus saying, "Someday you will understand, my child," and I smiled through my tears.

My belief that Christ would come again gave me deep reassurance and when the message came that Papa in Czechosolvakia had also died in that blessed hope, I could rejoice again: a few more years of waiting and aging and we would be together forever.

As for me, it was now time to take life a little easier and begin to enjoy the fruit of our hard work. I started to look around for a nice rocking chair. Yes, my cup was running over once again: the roses bloomed, the children seemed happy and well adjusted, and Rudy and I were very content with our daily routine at home, work, and church.

One evening I stood in my warm, golden, spacious kitchen, loading the dishwasher and enjoying the delight that this favourite gadget always gave me. My children sometimes claimed that we had bought the house because I had fallen in love with the modern dishwasher—and it was true that to me nothing else seemed to symbolize our good fortune and progress as much as that wonderful appliance did!

Into that scene of contentment stepped my husband.

"Honey, I've just had a phone call from Florida. The company wants to transfer us to Miami!"

"Oh, Schatzi, please don't accept. I don't want to leave this place—I love our new home and the neighbours. . . ."

"And your new dishwasher!" My husband raised one eyebrow and said no more.

I knew what he was thinking, and I thought the same but couldn't help but plead and beg: "Please, dear Jesus, please, let me stay. I am so tired of wandering, so tired of packing . . . I love it here so much!" But while I prayed and cried, I knew I could get no answer.

"Your will be done, God," I finally found the courage to pray, "and forgive me, Lord, if I have become spoiled or too attached to my house, the gadgets and the good life; make me willing to go where you want us to go!"

Is there such a thing as a sacrifice for God and his will? I thought I had made a sacrifice when I began packing. I felt sorry for myself while trying to be obedient, noble, and co-operative!

I am convinced that Jesus must have smiled while watching me grumble, wallow in self-pity, and give dutiful lip service to his will. For he had a surprise for me! Something so inaccessible I didn't even dare dream of it any more.

One of our main reasons for coming to the United States had been our dream of going to a Christian college, but after we saw how much it would cost we had buried those ambitions. We would have to concentrate on getting our five children educated instead. I packed to move to Florida, and three months later found myself moving to a college community in northern California instead. Rudy's transfer orders were changed and his boss permitted us to live in Angwin, a place where I had yearned to be for a long time.

All at once I found myself getting ready to go to college—and very scared! My U.S. citizenship made me eligible for a government defence loan, and the registrar granted me two years of undergraduate credit since I had taken courses here and there in the past years and also had proof of my years of teaching after the war in Germany. My oldest daughter, Chris, teased me:

"Mother," she chided, "don't you dare bring home a C in any subject. We expect your best at all times!"

Those words sounded very familiar! I hid my fears behind a self-confident smile. "Fine, kids, the race is on. Guess who is going to win?"

"Mother will," Rudy said, and winked at me. He beamed confidence and reassurance.

How does it look when a middle-aged woman with pigtails walks into a packed classroom of a hundred or more students—late—clutching her U.S. history book? This was a lower division class, attended mostly by freshmen, and I had the attention of every eye. The professor stopped for a long moment.

"There is a seat in the front row," he said pleasantly, and continued his lecture.

I started to take notes furiously but got bogged down fast.

Other students had a background of U.S. history: I had a dizzy head!

What was Plymouth? a car? a rock? a symbol?

What gave me the idea I could compete with bright American youngsters—and how had I thought I could go to college where they taught everything in English?

What would my children say if I flunked?

If I thought history was rough, my next course was rougher. Child development. It shouldn't be *that* hard. I could boast five-fold experience in that area—just common sense!

But I heard common sense expressed in a different vocabulary! I found out, when it was too late for second thoughts, that I didn't have an adequate English vocabulary for that class. But I had signed up for a loan and classes and there was no sense wasting time and money. I would make the best of it.

Then I was handed my first multiple-choice test. I had never laid eyes on such a monster before. German tests of my past had always been in essay form. My previous night classes had tested with quizzes, true and false tests, and by demanding reading reports which I could do.

After I had given that multiple-choice test one look of blank horror, I got up and put the paper on my teacher's desk and walked out without a word. I couldn't talk or I would burst into tears.

Good-bye, college dreams, I thought grimly. The whole deal would have been too good to be true anyway.

"Jesus," I prayed in utter dejection, "why did you bring me up here when you know me so much better than I know myself? You know that I can't take such horrible tests. The English language is impossible to learn, and I don't have enough background to catch on in the first place!"

"Go and see Dr. Hauptmann," Jesus seemed to say.

I marched into Dr. Hauptmann's office with the desperate

calm of a condemned person eating his last meal before execution.

Dr. Hauptmann, of Swiss-German descent, was not only a German professor but also a child psychiatrist. We had met the week before and I liked his jolly personality.

"Dr. Hauptmann, I shall drop out of college," I stammered the agitated announcement. "I can't do it!"

Dr. Hauptmann showed no surprise or shock. "Would you like to tell me why?"

"I don't know enough English." I broke down and cried. "I can't work out multiple-choice questions and I am terribly afraid that my memory will let me down again. I turn all blank when I get scared."

Dr. Hauptmann took a pencil and paper and drew a spiral. At the centre he put the word "anxiety". At the end of the circle line the word "failure". Then he explained.

"You are getting yourself into a vicious circle, Maria Anne. Your *Angst* (anxiety) pushes you towards inability to take tests or understand the meaning of a lecture. Now in order to unwind this spiral, which end would you have to pull off first?"

"*Meine Angst*," I said.

"Can you?" the doctor smiled.

"*Nein*," I said in desperation. "I tried but it gets worse from day to day."

"Okay then, let's try the other end."

"But I can't fail," I interrupted. "I would die with embarrassment."

Dr. Hauptmann nodded. "Look, you *are* ready to give up. What's there to lose? I want you to obey my doctor's orders and go back into the classrooms for the rest of the term and listen for the fun of it. Take the tests and see how *much* you can do right—for interest's sake only. If you fail I shall talk to your teachers and you always can withdraw up to a certain date. Will you do that for me since there is nothing to lose and it would be of value to me as a doctor to see the results? Stop being so proud and eager to make top grades. Go for the fun of learning!"

"*Ja*, I said and got up. If the man only knew how much I demanded of my children—now I would have to eat my own words!

I walked back to my child development teacher, an elderly, very kind lady, and apologized for walking out. She was so understanding it made me feel good.

"You may use your English-German dictionary when taking my tests; I trust you," she said warmly, "and I shall give you this first test orally."

Surprisingly enough, I knew most of the answers when she asked me, and I decided to obey Dr. Hauptmann! Even if I only learned something to benefit my own family it was worthwhile.

I didn't say much to my children, though. It would be soon enough to confess at the end of my first and last term, and hard enough to swallow my daughter's triumphant look when we compared report cards.

There was a text in my German Luther Bible, in the Psalms, which I loved but sometimes dreaded: "*Wenn Du mich demütigst, machst Du mich gross*" (When you humble me, you are making me great; Psalm 18:36).

I was surely at a great stage of my life if that text meant what it said. Too bad that the humbling part was so much more easily felt and observed by everybody than the greatness! But at the end of the term the only C was in U.S. history. Chris was very mature about it. "Don't worry about that C, Mother. I have one in P.E.!" She had my full sympathy. Both of us sighed with relief!

Later I heard Michael ask Chris, "You mean Mother didn't scold you for that C, Chris? What's wrong with her all of a sudden? She would have torn your head off last year!"

"Yes," Chris said, very grown-up, "but last year she didn't go to college, either; I hope she stays with it for a long time. They might even straighten her out yet! But don't get funny ideas for yourself, Mike. You'd better not take too many chances with your grades. You never know with her."

A year and two cut-off pigtails later, I donned the black graduation gown and that strange hat with the tassel, to march in with the seniors for graduation exercises. The world was a happy blur of sunshine, smiling faces, and wonder.

I was actually getting my degree, my Bachelor of Science, and my teaching degree from an American college!

After the ceremony, as I stood in the long reception line shaking hands and hugging people, Rudy walked up and laid a bouquet of long-stemmed red roses in my arms. He smiled so proudly I felt tears well up again.

What beautiful roses! But they looked a bit black in spots and were rather droopy. I motioned to Chris.

"Honey, what happened to the roses?" I whispered so that her father wouldn't hear.

Chris giggled. "When he brought them home he tried to hide them and get the petals freshened a bit, so he put the whole box in the freezer. Then he got so excited about getting all of us on time to the graduation he forgot the roses. They felt stiff when I got them. He wouldn't even have remembered to bring them. You know how Dad is."

I nodded and giggled and was deeply touched. I would never have graduated if he weren't such a kind, understanding husband and Chris such a dependable second mother in our family. This wasn't only my degree; it was a family accomplishment and belonged to all of us.

I said so during a celebration dinner that night and Rudy grinned. "That's okay, *Mammi;* you earned that paper, and we will all get our own. You don't have to share yours!"

I knew what he meant. I had promised Rudy that I would

take over the breadwinning after my graduation so that he could have his turn to go to college. We would pull each other to the degree of our choice.

"Rudy," I said very hesitatingly, "would you let me get my master's degree before we switch? I want to go into counselling so badly, and if I carry overloads I could make it in a year and a summer!"

Rudy smiled. "I expected that, little teacher; all you have been talking about lately is your wish to learn how to counsel better; I knew what you were up to for a long time—but we expect *only* good grades from you, Mother, no more C's. Your language handicap is no excuse!"

The children chimed in and were jubilant. At least they could stay another year and summer without the possibility of being moved away. They loved where we lived and had made many new friends.

I threw myself with new enthusiasm into my graduate studies and enjoyed most classes, but more than any class I enjoyed the association with my young fellow students. Our big rambling house on top of the hill became "Hirschmann Hill" to many young people and our place their home from home.

They enjoyed German *Kuchen*, potato salad, and other filling foods, but that special time of evening worship around the fireplace they obviously liked the best.

We sang a lot and talked. We argued and discussed. We prayed while forming a big prayer circle and always finished by reading my favourite chapter: 1 Corinthians 13, to me the definition of love in its highest form.

I wondered sometimes how much influence we really exerted and if our hospitality did any good. Was it just for our own benefit, since our whole family loved people? But one evening a sweet blonde girl who had never impressed me as a very religious girl said, "Stan and I are getting married," (they had met in our home) "and I asked the minister to base his wedding sermon on 1 Corinthians 13, the chapter I learned to love in your home!" I felt rewarded.

One boy left as a student missionary after the school year. When he came to say good-bye he looked into my eyes and said, "Someday when I start my own home I shall have worship time in my house just like you do. I will also open my house to young people. I realize we make much extra work for you—but I will never forget the hours around your fireplace!"

Such words brought joy and encouragement since I was aware that our house had become the object of gossip to some of our neighbours. Can anyone hang a light in the night without attracting bugs? Anyone was welcome and they knew it—even those with the bad reputations, and people whispered.

To know that Christ accepted people without discrimination became our comfort and strength. I learned more than psychology that year. I learned to do what seemed right to me and to defend young people, try to understand without judging—even the little old saints who were so quick with their tongues.

One afternoon shortly before my finals I struggled again with one of my hardest subjects, physiological psychology. All that memory work felt like a murderous threat to my poor brain. A lone college student had come to our house and sat on our front lawn in the shade of a bush. He had been around before but I didn't know him too well because he never talked. I felt a bit pressured and wondered if I should go out and welcome him, but decided to wait until he was ready to come in. I needed every minute for my studies.

"Go and talk to that boy!" Someone whose voice I knew very well by then spoke to me while I read aloud from my book.

"Lord," I said, "I have so much to study yet; could I talk to him later?"

"Go now," my friend Jesus said. "Right now!"

The boy was just leaving when I stepped out. "Don't leave, Jimmy," I called after him.

Hesitatingly the young man turned around. I stared, alarmed. His face looked haggard and his eyes so sad that my heart went out to him.

"Jim, for heaven's sake, what happened to you? Are you sick?"

"No," he said with a helpless shrug. "I am not sick. I am dead inside."

"Sit down, honey; let's talk for a while!"

We did. He talked and I listened. Like a waterfall his words tumbled out. His fiancée had sent the ring back and his world had come to an end; everything was broken forever.

"I haven't eaten for several days, Mum H." Most students called me that. "I can't get anything down. I want to die, and today I scraped enough pills together to do it. I decided to pray once more before I downed the pills, but while I talked to God it seemed that something impressed me to come to your house. I didn't want to come. That's why I didn't walk in. I thought if I had to come to you, you would come out and get me. I waited for you, then I decided to leave. But you didn't let me go away, did you?"

"Never mind, Jimmy," I said, shaken to the roots, "it's just that I have such a tough skull that even God sometimes has a hard time getting through to me. I *knew* I should come out and invite you in. I was too worried about a good grade to put you *first;* please forgive me!"

I got the boy into my kitchen and heated some soup and burned some toast—I felt that disturbed—and while I saw to it that he ate a few spoonfuls, I talked to him.

I told him that sometimes our greatest disappointments later become the solid foundations of great happiness for us. I shared some bits out of my life to prove the point, and Jimmy took it all in. Then we prayed together, and I asked him to promise me to flush the pills down the toilet.

"I will," he said solemnly, and I knew I could trust him.

I handed him a packed lunch for the evening, since he told me that he didn't feel able to go to the noisy cafeteria yet, and he walked away. I watched the slim, tall form of that young artist disappear and all I could say was, "Forgive me, Lord; forgive me for being so slow sometimes, so selfish! Isn't a person more than a good grade?"

The Lord must have smiled again, for I also got an A the next day.

That day I gave my Lord another promise. "Use my life to help troubled young people, O Jesus; I promise you that I shall go whenever you send me, regardless whether it is hard or easy, if it is pressure or joy; let me be a friend to the new generation, Jesus. Those kids need friends they can talk to. We adults are so busy with life, we are missing our highest calling that you, O God, gave to us; to feed your lambs, precious Shepherd! There are too many lost lambs around, too many lambs who need to be loved. Teach me to love them, all of them, dear Lord!"

I mean what I prayed and the Lord took me at my word. A year later my husband was at a university in southern California for graduate studies and I started to teach high school drop-outs. No more time to grow roses or to sit in a rocking chair, no dishwasher in our simple mountain home nor taking it easy—but happy? Oh, how could I be more happy! If ever my cup was running over it was now, for I had found my great and final calling. What more could my kind heavenly Father add to my new joy?

Sometimes falling stars drop out of our dream sky and become reality. Summer had come again and I was on my way to visit Germany. I had waited fourteen years for that moment and when it happened I thought myself dreaming.

My trip took me first to an Eastern university for a special workshop and then I was to go on to New York and fly across the ocean to Europe for three short weeks.

While still on that university campus I gave a talk one evening in one of the big dormitories and afterwards hurried to the door to get away before some listeners could corner me. Many unfinished assignments waited that night and I looked neither right nor left.

A little old lady stepped into my path and looked up.

"*Tante* Erhard!" I screeched with joy and hugged her closely. Who cared about assignments!

I did not know that she lived on that campus. Time and distance had interrupted our friendship; now we made the most of our reunion.

She owned a lovely little home with ruffled curtains, an old-fashioned rocking chair, and a tiny kitchen that smelled like mint.

We exchanged pictures. Yes, Chris was at college, Michael finishing high school. The two girls were young teenagers and Jo Jo a big boy and a football fan by now. Rudy was ploughing towards his Ph.D. in German philology at the University of California.

"Where did time go so fast?" *Tante* Erhard shook her grey head.

Her sons had finished school and married. One son was a minister, the other a college professor with a Ph.D in chemistry. I admired their lovely family pictures.

"Oh, *Tante* Erhard, God gave you the desires of your heart! I'm so happy for you!"

"God spared my sons for his service. I knew it all along," she nodded with motherly pride in her eyes.

"And what about—" I hesitated to say it.

"You mean my husband? Maria Anne, I have word from him! He is alive!"

I was so excited I couldn't talk, but motioned for her to tell me more.

One day I came home from work and saw a strange letter in

my mail. Before I opened it I knew already that it was a message from him. They kept him for twenty-five years in a *Schweigelager* (silent camp) in Siberia, Maria Anne! When they freed him he stayed in Siberia and started to look for us. One of our relatives in Russia knew that I had emigrated to the United States, so he wrote to the International Red Cross in Bern. They found our address for him and contacted us immediately; that foreign letter was from the Swiss Red Cross headquarters."

"Will he be permitted to come to America?"

"No, there is not much hope. I don't need to tell you why, do I? But somehow it doesn't matter. It is very hard to put it in words; we can write to each other and I can send him pictures and packages. The grandchildren are now the age our sons were when the war tore us apart, and now we are old and God has taught us patience. Soon, oh, so soon, we'll be united forever in his presence; what do a few more years on this old planet matter?"

"*Tante* Erhard," I said softly, "what would all of us do if we didn't have our blessed hope and the promises of God?"

"I would lose my mind, my dear. But there is a peace that passes all understanding, and God has given me that heavenly peace. I am content to trust him."

I remembered *Tante* Erhard's words when I stood at my mother's grave two weeks later.

All my bitterness came back to me but my foster sister comforted me. "For your sake it was better that you didn't come to Mother's deathbed. She was only a shadow of herself when she died. Her desperate struggle for every breath was agony for all of us who had to watch her. But her heart was in peace through all her suffering. She understood that you couldn't come so fast. You are privileged; you may remember her as she looked in her healthier days. Thank God for it—it's a happier memory!"

I thanked him. Yes, Jesus knew best!

In three weeks I whirled through all of West Germany and Austria but didn't dare to cross the border to see my beloved city. I wondered if I should, but my stepmother Bertha and my brother Rudy and sister Angelika protested strongly. We had never seen each other, my little brother Rudy stood a head taller than I and looked down at me. "Hi, big sister!"

I looked up. "Hi, little brother!"

They had come out of Czechoslovakia a few years after Papa's death, just before the Russians occupied the land of my childhood for the second time. Now they lived in West Germany.

We cherished every moment together and talked about Papa. Soon it was time for me to leave.

"Stay longer," my people pleaded.

"I can't. I must go home!"

"Didn't you come *home* to visit?" Angelika asked me.

"No, I am *going back* home and I can't wait," I said.

The big, silver bird hummed across deep waters through the night. "Make haste, jet bird! speed west. I long to go home, home to America!"

Rudy held me tight when I arrived at the airport. "I shall never let you leave us again!" he said.

"It was good that I went," I whispered into his ear.

"Why?"

I smiled through my tears. "Because I know now how it feels to come home!"